One Minute Food Manager

Manish Sharma

Published by Manish Sharma, 2023.

ONE MINUTE FOOD MANAGER

First edition. August 20, 2023.

Copyright © 2023 Manish Sharma.

ISBN: 979-8223736578

Written by Manish Sharma.

Table of Contents

One Minute Food Manager
A handy food lovers' guide for all world travelers

Let us come together and begin a journey of taste of foods across the globe.

By Manish Sharma

My Life mantra: Spread the sea of knowledge and raise the bar of wisdom globally.

Copyright: 2023: All rights reserved with Author.

To all professional colleagues to whom I shall always remain grateful for providing valuable inputs, based on this book is written.

ABOUT AUTHOR

A seasoned chemical engineer with Maser of science from BITS Pilani.

A Certified Six Sigma Black Belt.

CQI & RCA Qualified lead auditor for ISO QMS 9001, 14001, 45001, and FSSC 22000, IMS (Integrated Management System).

Diploma from IIP (Indian Institute of Packaging), Mumbai.

A Competent professional with over three decades of industry experience in flexible packaging, Labeling, Lamination, Chemical Production, Product Development, Project Management, Customer Relationship, Quality assurance, and Technical Services.

Skilled in the implementation of lean methodologies and 5S technique;

Hold competency in food packaging grade product legal and statutory compliance.

PREFACE

First edition
"Secret of success in life is to eat what you like and let the food fight it out inside."
Mark Twain

FMCG (Fast Moving Consumer Goods) food market is a broad category; we have chosen a wide range of products consumed daily by billions of people worldwide.

Health is one of the top prime priorities for every individual. Everyone wants to keep away from any disease.

We ensure that we have a good awareness of all kinds of products available in the global market.

Why This Book?

The purpose of writing this book is to help all food lovers across the globe to get at a glance handy foods, snacks, cookies, cakes & desserts, and pizza details within a minute.

The book covers various topics related to food safety hygiene, food supply chain, food safety challenges, a wide range of food products, food safety regulations, and one fascinating topic on the choice between vegetarian and non-vegetarian foods with pros and cons.

Please find this small pocketbook very useful.

Acknowledgment

Every completed task is the effort of so many peoples. This book is an example of this.

I am thankful to my wife and sons for supporting me throughout writing this book.

I am also thankful to my professional colleagues, from whom I got a lot of valuable practical experience that is now part of this book.

Information was collected from many sources such as the Internet, books, and newspapers, attending various training programs, visiting and interacting with customers, participating in the audit process, and addressing multiple technical issues during the three decades.

Since sources were not readily available for acknowledgment, I am grateful to everyone to be part of this journey for their direct or indirect support to make this task possible.

I am also thankful to all for using various illustrations /images to explain multiple concepts with more clarity better.

If any credit is missed or given inadvertently in the next version, it will be taken care of and brought to the Author's notice.

CHAPTER 1

Best Hygiene Practices> Let's be hygienic before eat

Compassion suits our physical condition, whereas anger, fear, and distrust harm our well-being. Therefore, just as we learn the importance of physical hygiene to physical health, we must know some emotional hygiene to ensure healthy minds.

Dalai Lama

Hygiene

The world has faced many pandemics in past years, and each one has created a panic situation across the globe.

We had overcome each challenge that came ahead of us.

In a fast few years, we have come across below challenges that have raised a significant threat to the life of human beings.

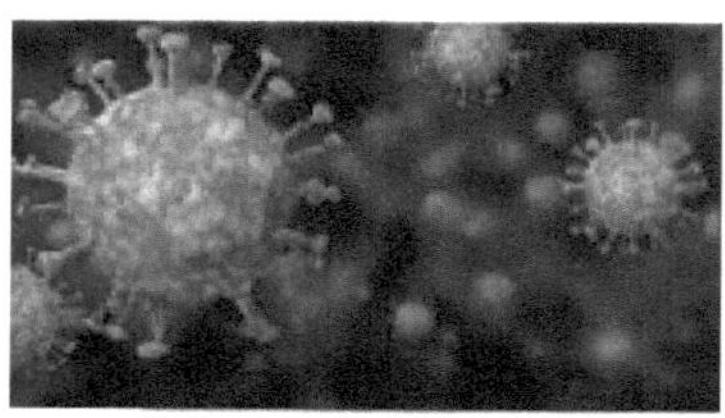

Anthrax in 2001

West Nile Virus in 2002

SARS in 2003

Bird flue in 2005

Ecoli in 2006

Swine flu in 2009

Ebola in 2014

Zika in 2016

Corona in 2019 current challenge, and strain in 2020

Everyone has the right to get good quality, hygienic, and safe products. Good hygiene practice is the requirement to ensure that food is contamination free.

Foodborne diseases could be due to the following reasons.

Poor sanitation conditions.

Lack of hygienic environment.

Our poor hygiene practices.

Sources of raw materials for food are unsafe.

Our storage and transportation conditions are not hygienic.

The source of the unhygienic condition could be biological, physical, or chemical contamination.

Biological contamination could be from viruses, bacteria, or parasites that could present in the air, water, animal, food, and humans.

Out of three, biological infection is critical as it is not directly visible, but its impact is enormous.

We have been following hygiene practices for years everywhere in the world.

Our old generation is teaching these practices, and it is handover to the next generation to continue.

Nowadays, when we are on the verge of a significant risk of life threat with pandemic diseases, it becomes very immediate attention for all of us globally to follow the best practices available globally to keep ourselves safe from any life-threatening lifestyle.

The primary issue that needs immediate attention is increased levels of chronic diseases, mental health, obesity in childhood, and the aging population.

BENEFITS OF: BEST HYGIENE PRACTICES

It enhanced best hygiene practices personally, socially, and at our professional working places.

It helps in improving the overall ability of the individual and organization to be safe while using or manufacturing food products.

It is a commitment of the individual, society, and organization to all the precautions everyone has taken to consider every hygiene aspect.

Good health and healthy products keep the cost of medication as well as the cost of unsafe food in the food supply chain.

Cleaning, maintenance, and hygiene helped in avoiding cross-contamination.

It helps in reducing infectious diseases.

It helps improve personal behavior like smoking, chewing, spitting, sneezing, coughing, etc.

It helps in improving the excellent working conditions.

It reduces food poisoning.

You are keeping yourself and your workplace clean.

Protect food from leading to illness or harm.

Increase in the morale of everyone.

Reduction in wastage of foods.

It helps destroy the harmful bacteria in the food while cooking or processing.

It prevents any bacteria that enter the foods from multiplying to the level that could result in ill health or spoiling nutrition in the early stage.

Good hygiene is the prevention of the growth of the bacteria.

Increase the shelf life of the product as well as maintain the best quality.

A good reputation helps increase the business.

It keeps away pests from the food hence reducing food poisoning and contamination.

Best hygiene practice No.1: Rise early in the morning, at least 90 minutes

before 

sunrise.

Best hygiene practice follows the total enjoyment of the nutrient quality of the food.

The surrounding environment during this time is in its purest form, with the maximum amount of fresh oxygen in the air, which rejuvenates our body with new energy.

As per scientific research during this period, there is the highest level of oxygen (41%) in the atmosphere, which is very beneficial for strengthening the lungs.

Meditation during this period exalted all the poisonous chemicals from our bodies to keep us away from diseases.

People feel healthy, strengthened, and energetic. These people energized themselves with the first ray of the sum that cures many diseases.

Exercise in the early morning removes all body and mind stagnation, helps in reducing fats, and there is overall body comfort, another advantage of the early rise is that it helps in lowering BMI (Body Mass Index) means low obesity, fewer chances of diabetes, depression, or insomnia.

Best hygiene practice No. 2: Namaste (greeting)

It is one of the most popular customs of India, followed from ancient times.

The meaning of this Namaste is that I bow to you and way of saying that may our mind is synchronized.

To perform Namaste, you must place the folded palms before your chest. It is the best hygienic way of greeting others, and to keep ourselves from such disease, we should also practice globally in the future.

Best hygiene practice No. 3: At home

During the defection or urination process, wasteful odor generates, and we should our hands with cow dung ash till it becomes odor-free, or we can also use soap. It ensures that any modern hand sanitization liquid should be free from scent or color. It helps in removing harmful bacteria as well as keeping you hygienic.

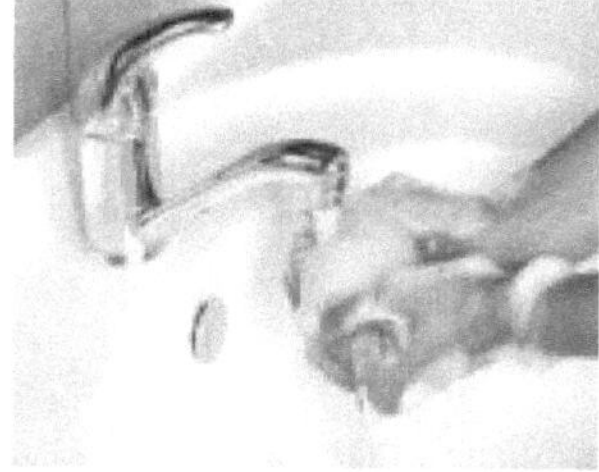

After that, there should be washing of feet and then rinsing of mouth as during the night sleep gas gets generated in our body that has to be removed by rinsing our mouth.

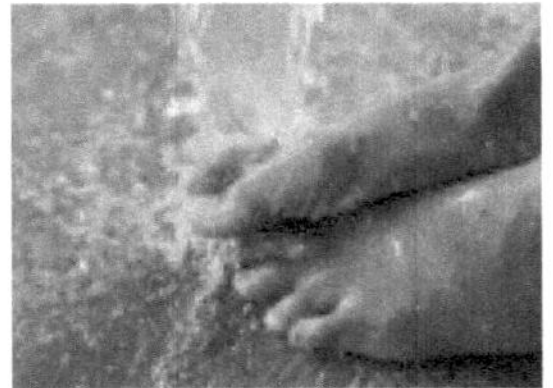

After that, we have to take water in a cupped hand to our face and eyes.

Regular cleaning of the teeth daily in the morning.

Take a daily bath early in the morning and wear well-washed, hygienic cloth before going for a morning breakfast.

Best hygiene practice No. 4: Fasting

In India, fasting has a long history; it is the country of yearly festivals. We celebrate with devotion, enthusiasm, and energy with social participation. God & Goddess are worshiped daily, along with a specific celebration.

There is a tradition of fasting during the festival to please the god or Goddess.

Primarily fasting is performed for 24 hrs, but it is subject to an individual's immune system for sustaining hunger and other medical constraints like blood sugar, etc.

The scientific reason for keeping fast is as under that is being followed for years.

It helps in controlling and steadily maintaining blood sugar by decreasing insulin resistance.

It helps in improving better health by reducing the level of inflammation.

It improves heart health, improving blood pressure, triglycerides, and cholesterol levels.

Due to less calorie intake, it helps in weight loss as well as enhancing metabolism.

It increases growth hormone secretion, which is necessary for metabolism, weight loss, and muscle strength.

It helps in delaying aging.

It promotes the detoxification of the body.

It helps in improving the immune system.

It reduces the probability of health risks due to cancer. It promotes the detoxification of the body.

It helps in improving the immune system.

This reduces the probability of health risk due to cancer.

Best hygiene practice No. 5: Eating with hands

In Western culture, people hardly eat their meals by hand.

A spoon, fork, and knife are the tools used for eating the food, which is considered a well-cultured table manners.

In India and many Asian countries, Greek and the Egyptians, We eat food by hand only; although it may not sound good to many people, there are many benefits of eating it by hand.

Our fingertip represents all five elements: air, water, fire, earth, and space. Our nerve ends at the fingertip help in boosting the digestion system.

The finger is heat sensitive, preventing the mouth from eating hot food.

It helps in eating slowly, which is good for digestion.

Traditionally right hand is preferred for eating food, and one must thoroughly wash hands with soap and water before eating. It is a hygienic eating process.

It enhances blood circulation.

When we eat food with our hands, health-friendly flora protects our digestive system from external exposure to harmful bacteria. Using spoons and forks might contain home microbes and other germs since it is kept on the table for a long time and exposed to the external environment, which may contain harmful bacteria.

One must wash his hands and mouth when he/ she finishes his food.

Eating by hand gives a sense of fullness early, helping to eat less and lose weight.

In another study, we saw that people using spoons, forks & knives, etc., eat very fast compared to people eating by hand may lead to blood sugar imbalance which may lead to type -2 diabetes.

It helps reduce obesity due to controlled eating because by eating by hand, you consciously know how much intake you are taking.

Best hygiene practice No. 6: Camphor an environmental sanitizer

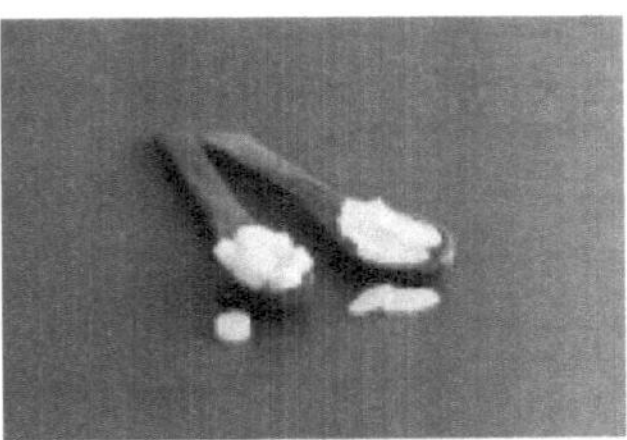

In Indian Hindu religious ceremonies, we have been using Camphor for years.

It is the last part of prayer when camphor candles and fumes spread in all the corners of the house.

The flame of the Camphor is Lord Shiva'sShiva's flame of consciousness.

From ancient times, it purified the air, and inhaling it has many medicinal advantages.

Camphor kills viruses and many other microbes.

Camphor is an active ingredient in the chest, muscular, and nasal ointment. It's another use as a moth and insect repellent.

Sometimes inhaling this and protecting against H1N1 (Swine flu virus) is suggested.

The substance present in this chemical is solid antiviral, antifungal, and anti-bacterial.

Best hygiene practice No. 7: Eating organic food
Fruits & Vegetable:

We produce organic food or food products without using any chemicals.

Chemical fertilizers, pesticides, and preservatives are not part of manufacturing organic food products.

Most of the population would like to know the benefits of organic foods, which is why it is more in demand and increasing daily.

Advantages of organic foods.

We have better overall health due to no use of pesticides and other chemicals.

The use of organic foods leads to the intake of more nutritious antioxidants that help prevent cancer, vision loss, heart disease, premature aging, etc.

Grazing natural grass by animals provides heart-friendly CLA(conjugated linoleic acid).

Non-organic food sources, especially livestock, and feeds, use antibiotics, vaccines, hormone growth, and animal byproducts to treat and feed animals. When humans consume these products, this excess dose directly impacts or weakens their immune system, leading to less defense against diseases.

Organic foods are tastier than conventional food because crops take more time to mature and have all nutrients, minerals, and sugar structures.

No pesticides in organic foods save us from diseases like cancer, weakened immune system, congenital disabilities, premature death, etc.

It is not a genetically modified product. The change in natural DNA produces GMOs (genetically Modified Products); this change might lead to slower brain growth, damage to internal organs, and thickening of the digestion system.

It helps in minimizing the environmental impact.

Organic foods are fresh as they do not have preservatives that enhance shelf life.

There are fewer chances of foodborne illness.

Organic food like milk has 60 % higher omega-3 fatty acids, vitamins, CLA, and antioxidants than no organic milk.

Organic food products have a deficient level of toxic metals.

Best hygiene practice No. 8: Drinking water hygiene quality

Water quality depends on pH, conductivity, minerals present, contaminations, etc.

Pure water is always odorless, tasteless, and colorless. It means good water should not have impurities like Total Dissolved solids (TDS); it is a measure of total ions, which makes water a good conductor of electricity.

Pure water is a bad conductor of electricity, but it is ideally not possible.

Drinking water is required to maintain good health; consumption varies per physical activity level, age, and environment-related issues.

As per WHO 2017 report, safe drinking water is a water source that does not create any significant threat to health when consumed over a lifetime, including different sensitivities that may occur during this period.

Benefits of good hygiene drinking water

As per science, we can not live more than 3~4 days without water.

Using clean water keep us safe from diseases and hence reduces medical bill.

It helps to maintain good health.

It helps to produce crops contamination-free so that no bacteria or diseases spread while consuming these food products.

Water used for agriculture should be from safe and clean resources.

We have many hygiene practices earlier in this post, where there is a need for using safe and hygienic water.

It provides nourishment. It is our life. Our body consists of 60% of water. Body hydration is mandatory for the effective working of the human organ system.

It helps in blood circulation by carrying oxygen and nutrients to each cell.

Unsafe water gives rise to diseases like Cholera, Typhoid, Hepatitis A, etc.

It helps in getting rid of all toxins from our bodies.

It improves sanitation because washing our clothes, body, and utensils and making our food with contaminated water will lead to diseases.

Best hygiene practice No. 9: Reduction in food wastage

Food wastage is the food that remains unused after a certain period or is used for consumption but completely not eaten and thrown away as waste.

A complete food supply chain takes approximately 150 days from seeding to the dining table, but we discard the food in less than a minute.

There is an excellent impact on the water, land, environment, and biodiversity due to the wastage of food.

Impact of food waste on health hygiene

With the increased population globally, household food waste generation is growing daily. Unattended waste is a significant threat, and health hazard leads to the probable spread of infectious diseases.

Unattended waste is an attractive destination for flies, rats, and other animals that helps spread diseases.

Typically wet waste releases a lousy odor that leads to unhygienic conditions, thereby significantly threatening health.

Best hygiene practice No. 10: Product those enhance the immune system

Many natural food products are available that help strengthen our immunity if these are taken regularly in our meals.

Current coronavirus (COVID-19) outbreaks have forced us to remain fit and enhance the immune system that helps us I am fighting against bacteria, viruses, and Pathogens.

These products are as under :

Citrus food:

Grapes food, Orange, Lemon, etc., are excellent sources of Vitamin C. It helps enhance white blood cells level in our body.

Broccoli:

It contains Vitamins A, C & E, Minerals, fibers, and antioxidants. It is one of the healthiest food products.

Garlic:

It helps fight infection, reduces blood pressure, slows arteries' hardening, and boosts the immune system due to the sulfur-containing compound Allicin.

Ginger:

It helps in the reduction of inflammation which cures sore throat and nausea. It also helps in the removal of chronic pain and cholesterol.

Spinach:

It is high in vitamin C. It is a good antioxidant and contains Beta carotene, which keeps our skin and eye healthy.

It also helps reduce infection; it is always recommended not to cook thoroughly so that other nutrients get released from oxalic acid.

Yogurt:

It is rich in Vitamin D that is a natural defense against diseases.

Almond:

It helps in fighting against the cold. Half a cup of almonds is sufficient for the daily requirement of Vitamin E, as it strengthens the immune system. It is a fat-soluble vitamin because it requires fats to absorb Vitamin E.

Turmeric:

It is an anti-inflammatory compound in treating Osteoarthritis, and rheumatoid arthritis.

Green/ black tea:

Both contain flavonoids which are antioxidants. Green tea also contains Epigallocatechin Gallate (EGCG), an antioxidant that helps improve immune function. It is also a good source of an amino acid (L theanine) that helps produce a compound in T cells that fights germs.

Papaya:

It is rich in Vitamin C. One whole papaya gives more than a day's body requirement of Vitamin C.

It also contains the digestive enzyme Papain which has an anti-inflammatory effect. It also contains Potassium, Vitamin B, and folate, which is beneficial for overall health.

Kiwi:

It contains Folate, Potassium, Vitamin K, and Vitamin C which helps in improving the white blood cell level to fight with infection.

Sunflower seeds:

It is a good source of phosphorous, magnesium, Vitamin B6, and Vitamin E, potent antioxidants. Vitamin E improves the immune system.

Back to top

CHAPTER 2

Food Safety Challenges >Basic concept of food safety

Let your food be your medicine, and your medicine be your food.
<u>Hippocrates</u>[1]

FOOD SAFETY CHALLENGES

Basic Understanding

Nowadays, it is a growing trend of food outings or less preparation of food at home due to other superseding priorities and commitment, which restrict individuals with no option other than looking for ready availability of ready-to-eat food products within a shorter time and doorstep delivery, for example, Zomato, Swiggy, Pizza hut, Domino, and many more around the world.

---

1.   *https://www.azquotes.com/author/22138-Hippocrates*

It has added a lot of food safety challenges due to the uncontrolled source of incoming raw materials and their quality.

Food Safety Concept

Now let us understand Food safety challenges more elaborately:

Food Safety is generally referred to the proper handling, preparing, and storage of food in the best possible way to minimize the probability of individuals falling sick from food-borne diseases.

Food safety is now a concern for everyone globally, covering a wide variety in many different sections of everyone's life.

Predominantly, it aims to prevent food from getting contaminated and cause food-related issues, such as food poisoning.

Different methods and techniques achieve it. For example, properly cleaning, sanitizing all contact surfaces, processing equipment, and other pots.

Implementing best hygiene practices, effective pest control systems, and a safe work environment are the key to success in food safety.

Major Challenges

> Change in lifestyle
> Evolving biological risks
> Challenges associated with processed and pre-packaged food
> Inadequate literacy level about nutrition & food safety
> Excess consumption of nutrients or other food ingredients
> Increased consumer dependency on digital services or dietary choices
> Food-fraud
> Food-defense
> Bioterrorism
> Imported food products.
> Climatic change.

> Increasing the concentration of the supply chain
> Food allergen

Let's discuss and understand each global challenge.

Change in lifestyle

In the present world, we spend much more of our days feasting out at cafés than we did previously. In the old generation, eating out would probably be an uncommon treat; put something aside for exceptional events.

Nowadays, numerous families are eating out on a weekly or some time before that. Furthermore, you'll probably accumulate more calories when you eat out than at home.

This expanding pattern of eating out is growing; people are becoming more overweight and inviting health-related issues.

Evolving biological risks

Out of four significant hazards, e.g., Physical, chemical, biological, and allergen, biological is one of the major concerns as it can not be detected directly by the naked eye.

We can classify biological hazards by the contamination of microorganisms in food items.

It is present in the air, food, water, animals, and the human body; these harmful microorganisms create food-borne diseases.

There are various types of biological hazards found in multiple products

Salmonella: Meat, Poultry, juice, fruit, eggs, unpasteurized milk, cheese, fruits, vegetables, nuts, and spices.

E.coli: Uncooked fruits, vegetables, meat, unpasteurized milk, cheese, etc.

Norovirus: RTE (Ready to eat) foods, shellfish, etc.

Listeria: Hot dogs, Ready-to-eat deli meats and hot dogs, unpasteurized milk or juice, unboiled milk.

Campylobacter: Raw and undercooked poultry, unpasteurized milk, contaminated water.

Challenges associated with processed and pre-packaged food

Buying processed foods leads to individuals eating more than the suggested measures of sugar, salt, and fat as they may need to learn what amount is in the food they are purchasing and eating.

These foods can likewise be higher in calories because of the high measures of included sugar or fat, high in sugar content.

- The product packaging is designed for excess consumption.

- Artificial ingredients are added to the product to enhance shelf life and taste.

- People are becoming habitual with junk food.

- The product generally contains high carbohydrates.

- The product has low nutrient content.

- The product has low fiber content.

- It is easy to digest.

- It contains high transfats

If these are in products, it leads to increased obesity and illness.

Inadequate literacy level about nutrition & food safety

It is one of the significant challenges globally to have a low literacy level on nutrition and food safety.

There is a proper need for communication about health communications and health literacy, affecting consumer knowledge and behavior regarding food safety, nutrition, and other health matters.

Food literacy in other broader contexts is food well-being; it provides physical but also emotional and psychological nourishment.

Knowledge about food safety requirements will improve the quality of consumption choices.

There are three basic requirements, i.e., Conceptual knowledge, Individual level literacy, and motivation for active participation.

Excess consumption of nutrients or other food ingredients

some ingredients are extra in many foods, including breakfast cereals and beverages. Due to that, we take more than prescribed; the excess is only sometimes ok as one side is more expensive, and there is every chance of side effects.

Excess of Vitamin A causes liver damage, bone weakening, headache, etc.

Excess Omega-3 fatty acids intake creates blood thinning problems.

An excess amount of cinnamon contains coumarin, which may be harmful if taken in excess.

Nutmeg provides flavor to meals, but when used in excess may cause poisoning.

The active ingredient in regular coffee is caffeine, but an intake above 400 to 600 mg may cause overwhelm the nervous system, causing insomnia, nervousness, and irritability.

Brazil nuts contain selenium, but excess intake could be toxic.

So it is necessary to take nutrients and other food ingredients as prescribed only to avoid any side effects which might turn into a severe health concern.

Food fraud

Food fraud is the demonstration of deliberately adjusting, distorting, mislabeling, substituting, or altering any food item anytime along with the farming to the dining table.

Misrepresentation can happen in the raw material or call it ingredients, in fixing, in the final food product, or the food packaging.

Deliberate substitution, weakening or expansion to a raw material or food item, or distortion of the material for monetary profit (by expanding its evident worth or lessening its expense of generation) or to make hurt others (by noxious tainting) is 'Food fraud.'

Food fraud is the trickiness of buyers through the deliberate deformation of food.

- By substituting one item for another.

- Utilizing unapproved upgrades or added substances

- Distorting something (e.g., nation of source)

- Misbranding or forging

Food defense

It is the procedure adopted to prevent any malicious interference of foreign objects in raw material or final product that harms health.

It protects food products from intended contamination by physical, biological, chemical, or any radiological introduction to cause harm.

Food defense is the better word is intentional contamination by any company or competitor employee for damaging the company's brand image, causing large-scale product recall and financial trouble, but no intention to create mass-scale public illness.

People of this kind are aware of product manufacturing procedures and know the CCP (Critical Control Points); failure to comply leads to a mess.

Bio-terrorism

It is the intentional contamination of harmful bio-organism in food products to affect humans or some other living body at a large scale, termed bioterrorism.

The intentional release of viruses, bacteria, or other germs in food products leads to sick or killing people, livestock, or crops.

It would not be wise to share any such type of detail. Imported food products.

Importers must ensure that foreign suppliers who manufacture the food products comply with all food safety-related legal requirements for exporter and importer nations.

The following are essential requirements for importing food products to ensure good quality.

- License/Registration required for import of food.
- Shelf Life of Imported Food
- Packaging and Labeling of Imported Food
- Food Sampling and Analysis, no objection Certificate/ Non-conformance Certificate

Climatic change

Climate change is impacting food safety resulting in malnutrition. Safe and utterly nutritious food is vital in addressing this issue.

Another impact of climate change on the availability of secure food is being discussed on the global platform and is an area of interest for research.

Microorganisms like bacteria and viruses can survive at higher temperatures and humidity levels and grow exponentially.

Many food-borne pathogens like Salmonella grow very fast in such favorable climatic conditions.

There is an emergence of new biological hazards due to frequent changes in crop technology to improve productivity.

Pathogen is becoming more and more antibiotic-resistant due to the use of medicine for farm animals.

Nowadays, the use of various range of chemicals in crop manufacturing processes creates a wide range of food safety issues due to the presence of toxins.

If we see at ocean aquaculture, there is a significant risk of a high concentration of bio-toxin in fish. After consumption, it would finally impact the health of the human being.

Increase in concentration of the food supply chain.

The concentration of the food supply chain is on a growing trend. Major players are controlling most of the commodity FMCG products with a significant pie of their share in the global market.

For example, three to four players control around 40 % coffee market. In contrast, a similar no. of companies, in comparison to millions of producers and consumers on either side of the chain, controlled 70 to 80 % of tea globally; the same applies to food and beverage, confectionery, etc.

There is also the domination of food retailing by Supermall like Walmart, Metro, and many more.

Food safety and traceability requirement has shifted control production operation to the extensive farming house.

For lowering manufacturing costs, there is a probability of compromising with environmental precautions in disposing of waste material produced or looking towards employing cheaper labor.

It creates a lot of risk and uncertainty that producers could act to downgrade product quality or decrease research and innovation exercises due to a lack of funds.

Legal bodies globally have taken several initiatives to address this excessive buying power for the benefit of farmers /producers.

Food allergens

Allergens are mostly proteins base substances that naturally occur in foods, and their derivatives may cause grave concern to the immune response system.

When our immune system attacks protein, it is termed a food allergy. Our method produces a protein called IgE antibodies which fight food allergens.

When anyone intakes this food again, our immune system uses this antibody to fight against this allergen.

The European Union prepared a detailed list of allergens that identifies as wheat, rye, barley, oats, kamut, crustaceans, eggs, fish, peanuts, soybeans, milk, nuts, for example, almonds, hazelnuts, walnuts, cashews, pecan nuts, Brazil nuts, pistachio nuts, macadamia nuts and Queensland nuts, mustard, and sesame seeds.

Japan has declared allergens are eggs, milk, dairy products, wheat, buckwheat, shrimp/prawn, peanuts, salmon roe, soybean, kiwi, banana, crab, chicken, tree nuts, squid, mackerel, meat, salmon, gelatin yam, and peach.

TECHNICAL DICTIONARY

Here is the description of terms underlined in blue.

Food fraud: All the live animals that grow to produce food products are called livestock. For example, Cow, Goat, Pig, Chicken, etc.θ

Food defense: It is the growing of water animals such as fish or plants in the water.

Back to top

CHAPTER 3
Most Popular Snacks From Around the World

"Your diet[1] is a bank account. Good food choices are good investments"
   Bethenny Frankel

A snack is a small meal generally taken between lunch and dinner. Snacks have a wide range, including packaged and processed foods; we cook at home too.

---

1. *https://food.ndtv.com/health/the-whole30-diet-just-a-fad-diet-taking-the-internet-by-storm-or-something-substantial-1442414*

Having small meals or, precisely, snacks at frequent intervals in a day is one of the finest ways to keep your higher energy level even when you are very busy with your business activities.

The selection of healthy food consists of vitamins, minerals, and nutrients that will energize your body and keep your worrying health parameter, for example, blood sugar, consistently within the defined limit.

Eating healthy snacks is better than overeating heavy lunch or dinner.

Occasional high dozing of food is a good practice. Healthy snacks full of protein and others are very good for you and keep this mid-afternoon discomfort at the bank.

Then what could be good quality snacks?

It should be effortless to make, excellent taste, and fill you, keeping your BMI (Body Mass Index) in line to keep you fit and energetic.

Snack foods are designed in such a way that they can be easy to carry, very fast to make, and fulfilling the needs.

Processed snack foods have more shelf life, which means extended durability and convenience than prepared food.

This product may contain preservatives and flavors to suit the requirement of consumer taste.

Globally snack food market is categorized into different geographical zones.

North America

When we visit any shopping store or supermarket, we find an abundant supply of snack products, and choosing the right quality of healthy snack foods becomes challenging.

Without a doubt, you have seen some of the delicious snacks and chips on every television channel or movie media, so why don't you try some of them for yourself?

Due to business globalization, many of us have to visit around the world and being abroad, there is a probability of favorite snack food sickness; everyone who visits misses their favorite food, and if it is a long tour, it would not be possible to carry along with you.

Overseas, you might have tried many local dishes and found them delicious and tasteful, but it would not be easy to go away from the taste you developed from growing age.

Many of the snacks readily available in the US are very hard to find in other countries, for example, cream cheese, peanut butter, pretzels, and many more, and if you find them by hard effort, they would be too costly.

Here we are come up with the most popular snack in North America:

- Potato chips
- Popcorn
- Crunchy cheese
- Pretzels
- Crispy rice treat
- Corn chips
- Salty Combo of cereal, pretzel, and breadsticks with many flavor
- Fruit Gushers
- Wide range of pudding
- Taste of mix salt andsweet : Peanut with raisins,Yogurt covered raisins.
- Creamy peanut butter
- Oatmeal
- Sandwich creamy peanut butter in grain base biscuit
- Roasted and then salted pistachios a sweet, and salty combinations.
- Protein-packed snacks
- Cereals for small kids, and infants.
- Combo of cheese, almond, and apricot
- Combo of Chocolate & vanilla ice creams with cookie dough,

and brownies.

South America

As we have seen above, people in North America enjoy a wide range of snacks. Still, apart from these, some specialty snack food is very popular in South America, which are mouth-watering and made with a traditional method. Those who are a food lover and visiting these countries would get an opportunity to taste them.

Empanadas from Argentina

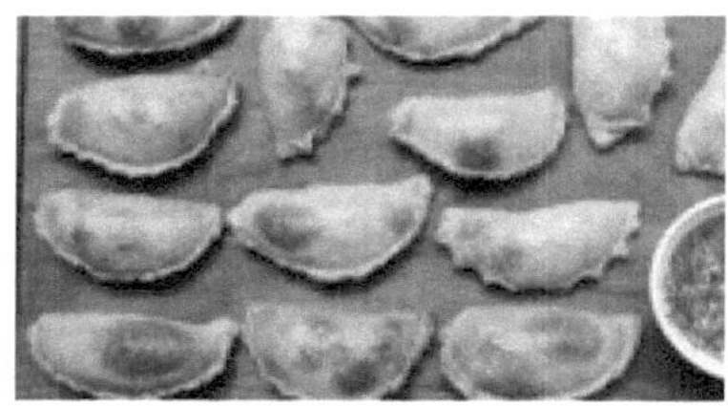

It is the stuff of meat, vegetables and potatoes in combination with fish also. In other variety with egg, chicken, ham and cheese.

Croquetas from Spain

It is the stuff of thick bechamel and croquetas.

Ceviche from Peru

It is a dish made from raw fish cured with citrus and served with Corrianded Onion and red chili.

Arepas from Venezuela and Colombia

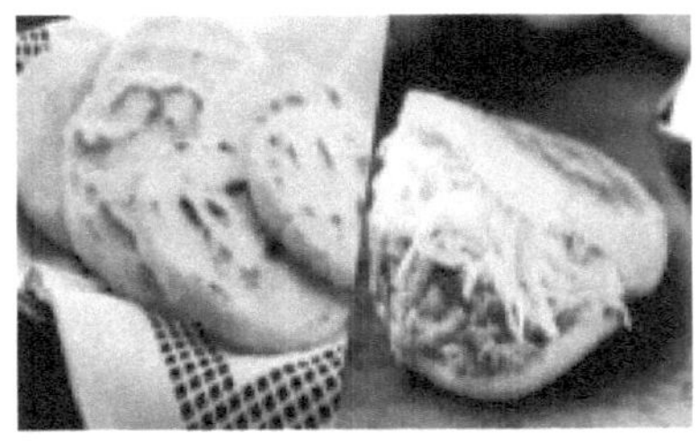

Patty is stuffed with cheese, avocado and vegetables.

Tequeño from Venezuela and Colombia

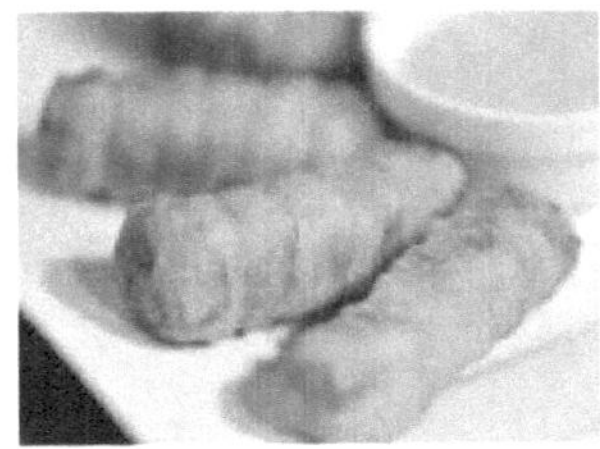

Tequeños is fried bread along with cheese sticks filled with lighter cheese.

Fugazza from Argentina

It is a basically a baked cheese roll.

Brigadeiro from Brazil

It is a dessert made with condensed milk using cocoa, chocolate, and butter.

Adding to this list are some of the more popular snacks.

Arrumadinho a Brazilian item

Coxinha

Brazil's favorite street foods.
Medialunas

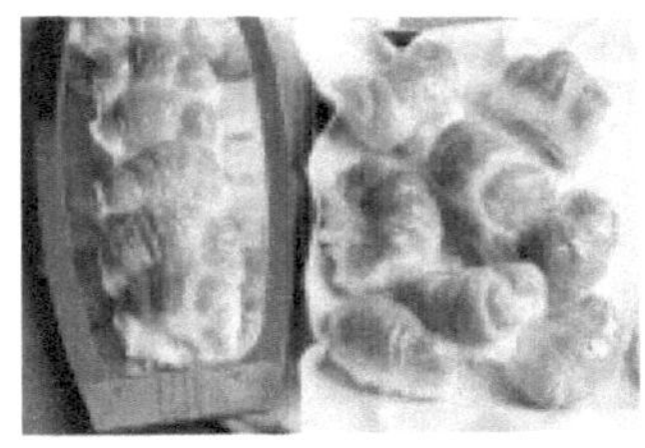

An Argentinian food
Pastels

A snack from Brazil
Papa Rellenas

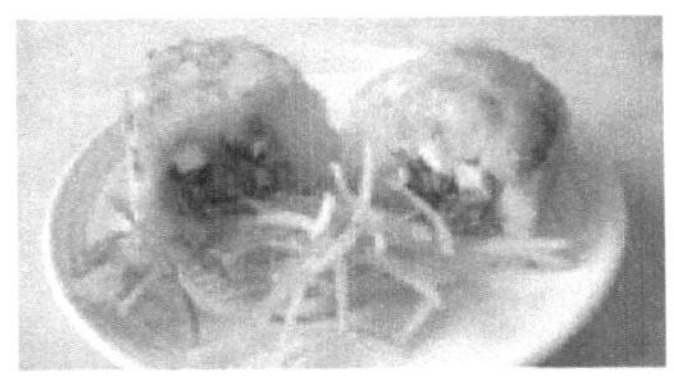

A traditional Peru food.
Saltenas

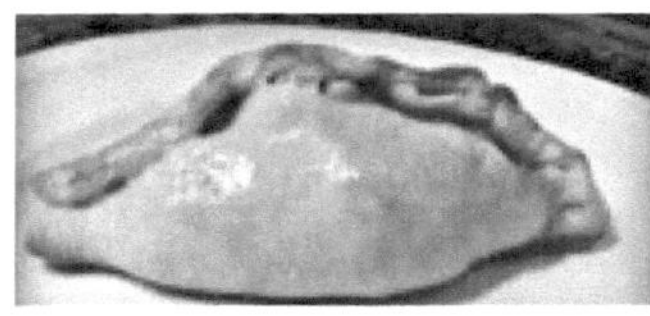

A snack from Bolivia

Sandwiches de miga

From Argentina
Lampreado

From Paraguay
Chapa

Popular snack from Chile

Aborrajado

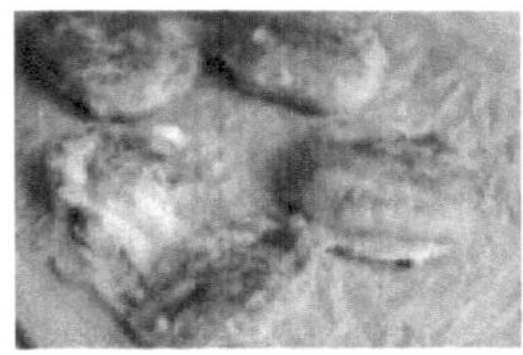

It is a Colombiansnack.

Europe

Europe is a big continent comprised of more than 40 countries. It offers a wide range of snacks globally.

Supermarkets and other retailers in Europe are now keeping more healthy snacks due to the snack industry observing a broad change in adopting the healthy snacking approach.

New trends are getting emerge in the European snack food market.

European snack foods. Each has its taste, flavor, and uniqueness and is very popular across the globe.

The internet has opened many doors to explore great delicious European snack treats.

Crocchè from Italy

This Italian snack is consisting of eggs, parmigiano, cheese, mashed potatoes, prosciutto, and salami.

Pirukas from Estonia

This snacks is made from dough filled with pastry, meat, ham, carrots, mushrooms, cabbage, and rice.

Bocata de atún from Spain

It is a Spanish bocadillo sandwich made with baguette and canned tuna in oil.

Frikandel from Belgium

It is a deep fried sausage snacks.
Utopenci from Czech

It is a combination of sausages, bay varieties of spices
Bulviniaiblynai from Lithuiania

This golden color dish is consisting of grated potatoes, eggs, flour, salt, onion, pepper and lemon juice.
Pampushki from Ukrain

This is combination of dough with flour, eggs, butter, oil, salt, milk, fruit jam, berries, and cottage cheese.
Smažený from Czeck

This cheese based dish is made with eggs, breadcrumbs, and flour, and finally fried till it becomes crispy.
Pain aux raisins from France

This is consisting of buttery dough or sweet bread dough , raisins, and crème pâtissière.

Plackiziemniaczane

:

It is a potato pancake made with grated potatoes and onions, along with eggs.

Milhofrito from Portugal

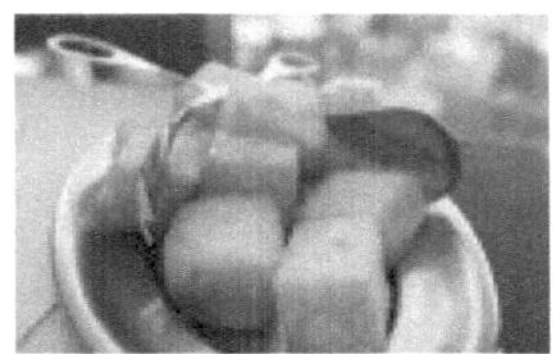

This snack is consisting of fried small piece of cornmeal sliced cabbage, garlic, and other herbs.

Zwiebelkuchen from Germany

It is a onion cake made with made with yeasted dough, smoked bacon, and a mixture of eggs and sour cream.

Chiftele from Romania

This is a meatballs consisting of bread crumbs, mashed potatoes, minced meat or chicken, onion, parsley leaves, garlic and lovage.

Paszteciki from Poland

It is a pastry made with buttery dough, mushrooms, cabbage, or minced meat.

Thissnack is consisting of phyllo dough that is filled with feta cheese and eggs.

Pogácsa from Hungary

Pogacsa is a small round pastry.It is found in wide varieties of potatoes, cheese, bacon, pumpkin seeds, and cabbage.

Oliebol from Netherland

It is deep fried fried dough made with flour, eggs, milk, baking powder, and yeast.

Kibbeling from Netherland

This snack dish is made with deep fried fish pieces, that is dipped in batter and served along with garlic, ravigote, and remoulade sauce.

Apaki from Greece

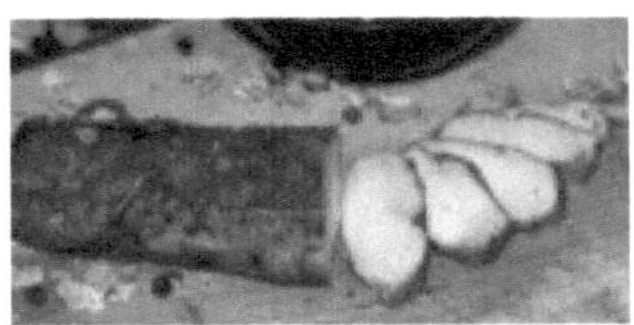

It is made with smoked meat loin and combination of herbs such as marjoram, sage, thyme, and oregano.

Bitterballen from Netherland

Thissnack is consisting of deep-fried, bread-crumbed, meat-filled balls.

Kartoffelpuffers from Germany

This is a flat round crispy golden fried thick batter that consists of grated raw potatoes, flour, and eggs.

Pastizz from Malta

This is a pastry filled with ricotta, peas, ricotta, anchovies, meat, or apples.

Bublik from Ukrain

This is a yeasted bun that is before baking poached in water sprinkles with sugar, sesame and poppy seeds.
Taralli from Italy

It is a bagel-shaped dough ring, that is prepared from olive oil, flour, salt, pepper, and fennel seeds.
Knäckebröd from Sweden

Thissnack is acrisp-bread.
Patatasbravas from Spain

It is a potato cubes dipped in a spicy tomato sauce along with onions, chili powder, garlic, and paprika.

Asia Pacific

Major countries in this region are India, China, Japan, Australia, South Korea, and New Zealand.

Asia Pacific region is emerging as a growing salty snack market globally; China is leading from the front.

With a wide range of flavors and food traditions, the Indian snack market is growing.

Let us see some country-specific most popular snacks.

India

Chakli or Murukku

It is a tasty tea time snack made from rice and lentil mix flour.

Salty NamakPare

It is one of the most famous tea-time snacks in India.
ChatpatiAlooChaat

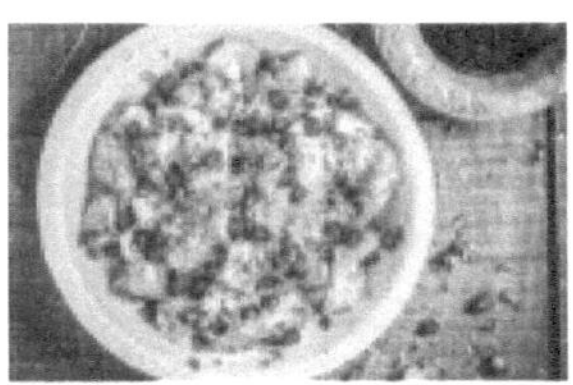

Spicy potato dish.
Kachori

Most favorite tea-time snack of India, Kachoris are deep-fried bread. It has wide varieties also.
DahiBhalla

The most loved street snack of India, particularly North India consists of curd and lentil base bada.

Bread Pakora

The undisputed king of salty snacks, hard from outside but soft from inside.

Home-made Panipuri

The most famous street snack of India. It consists of spicy water inside fried thin bread.

Mixed Sprouts Corn Chaat

Healthy food consists of proteins, Vitamin K, dietary fiber, Vitamin C.

Chicken kebabs

It is served with mint sauce.

Fried Banana chip

It is a south India snack especially from kerala.

Khaman

It is a very light, soft, spongy, snack prepared from ground gram flour and garnished with green chilies, coconut, and coriander leaves.

Vadapav

This is made from mashed potatoes, mixed with chilies, coriander, and spices and dipped in chickpeas flour deep-fried and then put in between Buns.

Handvo

A traditional Gujarati cake, made with lentils, rice, and buttermilk.
Poha

One of the most no spicy popular snack of North India. flat rice roasted with onions, curry leaves, green chilies, pomegranate, and peanuts.
Momos

From Tibet but very popular in India.
Masala Papad

It is a crispy tortilla chip made of black gram, and served with sliced tomato, onion, coriander and spice.
Bombay Mix

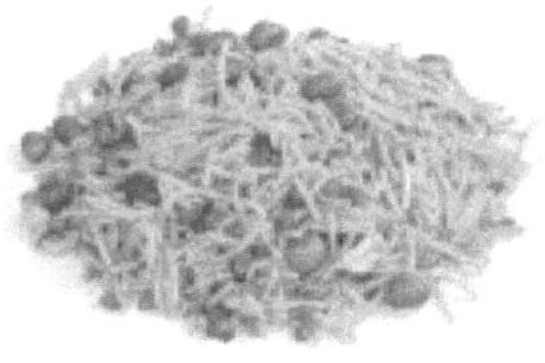

It is a blend of dried ingredients, like chickpeas, lentils, sev, peanuts, and spices.
China
Rose cake

It is made of a puffed rice paste that crumbles and stuffed with a rose.
Mahua

Very crispy twisted donuts.
Bingtanghulu

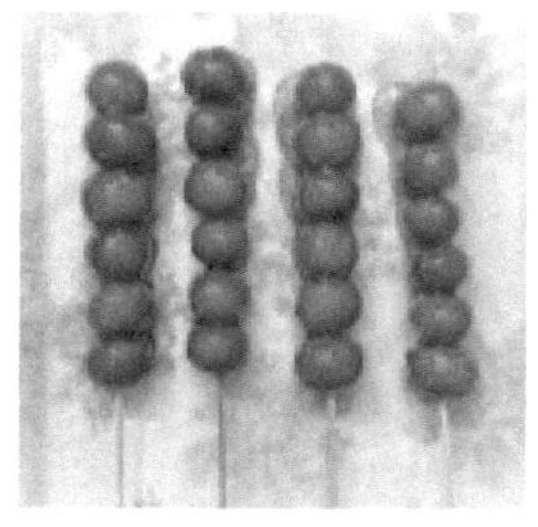

It is hawthorn berries skewers with icing sugar.
Stinky tofu

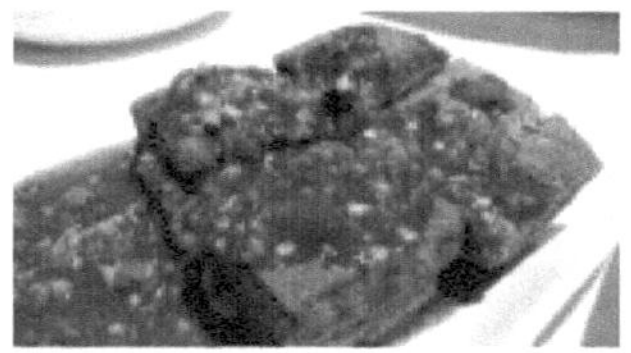

It is a deep-fried fermented bean card.

Rice rollers

Yang rouChuan:

It is a mutton skewer which is popular in china.

Youtiao

Fried bread sticks are served with porridge, soymilk.
Dried squid

Curry fish balls

Steamed bao buns

Nian Gao

It's a delicious glutinous rice cake.
   Japan
   Konsome

Popular seasoning for a snack is konsome, or consommé, a clear soup made from a richly seasoned stock of meat and vegetables.
   Kappa Ebisen

Crunchy shrimp flavored chips, made from wheat flour.
   Crepes

Some will argue that crepes aren't a Japanese original idea, and they might have borrowed the original idea from the French. ...

Dorayaki

These are red-bean filled with a pancake.

Manjū

It is a famous traditional Japanese candy.

Dango

It is a sweet dumpling made from Mochiko (rice flour).
Daifuku

It is a Japanese confection consisting of a small round mochi stuffed with a sweet filling.
Australia
Meat Pies

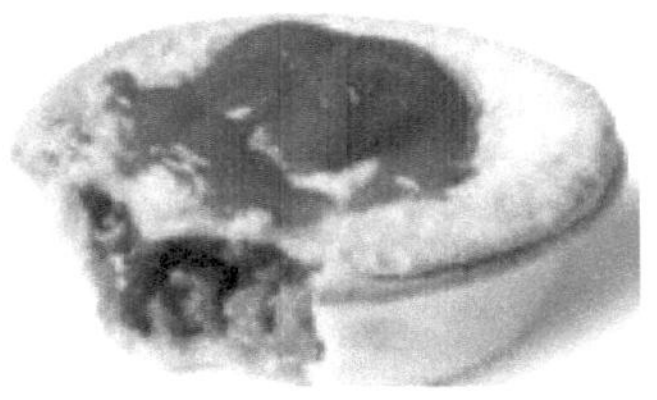

Most popular snacks of Australia
Anzac Biscuits

Chicken Parmigiana

Pavlova

A meringue cake base topped with whipped cream and fruit.
Aussie barbecue

It is with sausages, burgers, steak, fresh seafood, bread and tomato or barbecue sauce.

Barramundi

It is the Aboriginal name for this type of sea-bass found in Australia.

Lamington

It is a square of sponge cake covered in chocolate sauce or sometimes raspberry sauce and then covered in coconut.

Thailand

Coconut Pancake: kha nom krok

Thai BBQ Skewers

Thai Crepe: kha nom bueng

Thai Japanese-Style Crepe: Khanom Tokyo

Northeastern Thai Sausage saikrokissan

Indonesia
   PisangGoreng (Fried Bananas)

NangkaGoreng (Fried Jackfruits)

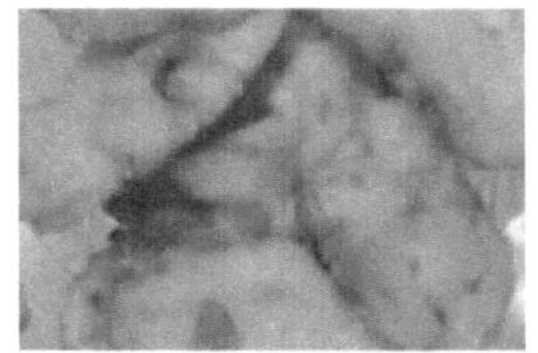

Tape Goreng(Fried Tape)

Tahu Isi (Veggies-Filled Tofu)

TahuBakso (Meat-Filled Tofu)

Mendoan

BakwanJagung (Corn Fritters)

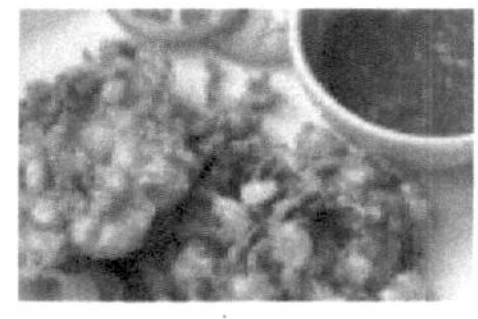

PerkedelKentang (Potato Patties)

SingkongGoreng (Fried Cassava)

Philippines
Banana-cue

Local banana called "saba" is coated with brown sugar, deep-fried in oil and skewered on a stick a la barbecue.

Kwek-kweks

This is hard-boiled quail eggs coated with orange batter and deep-fried.

Fish Ball

Snack is a round, fish-flavored dough that is deep-fried in a wok.

Tahos

This is warm, fresh soft bean curd with a richer volume sweetened with caramelized brown sugar syrup.

Pinaypay

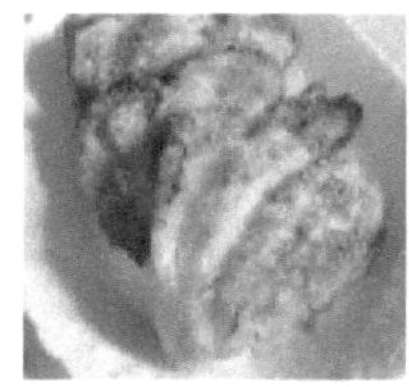

Bananas are divided then coated in flour with achuete, deep-fried, and sprinkled with white sugar.

Lumpiangtogue or mung bean sprout spring rolls

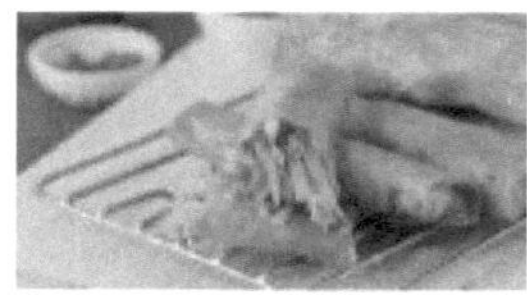

This is fried vegetable spring roll, lumpiangtogue is stuffed with sautéed mung beans rolled in egg wrapper, and then fried.

Chicharonbulaklak

This is made from chicken omentum.

Dynamite or dinamita

Dynamites are green chilies wrapped in egg rolls and stuffed with meat and cheese slices and deep-fried.

Middle East

Turkey,Iraq, Saudi Arabia, Yemen, Syria, UAE, Israel, Jordan, Palestine, Lebanon, Oman,Kuwait, Qatar, Bahrain are countries fall in the Middle East of the world.

Find below some of the popular snack foods of the Middle East.

Honey spiced nuts

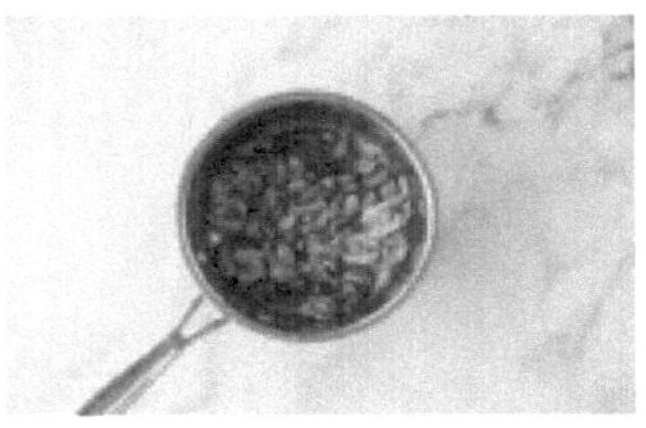

A combination of cinnamon, ginger, nutmeg, cardamom, salt, and sugar.

Crunchy roasted cumin chickpeas

It is served with cumin, paprika and coriander.

White beans Hummus Hummus

It is made with chickpeas.

Pita chips

Pita chips are delicious and strong to hold with the thickest of hummus dips.

Middle eastern pita taco

It is also packed with chicken, cheese, vegetables, and a flavorful sauce. It uses a bunch of cilantro.

Cardamom pistachio shortbread cookies

Shortbread in the Middle East known as Ghoraibi, spiced with cardamom, scented with rose water, and topped with almonds.

Cheesecake baklava

The phyllo dough, which is a main ingredient of baklava, serves as a crust for a cheesecake, and topped with honey syrup and chopped pistachios.

Grilled halloumi

Mini-slabs of chewy goodness are made from goat and sheep milk.

Falafel

Fried chickpeas with herbs a delicious snack.

Tabouleh

A combination of bulgur, parsley, mint, onion, and tomatoes.

Fattoush

Crispy lettuce, crunchy fried squares of pita, diced tomatoes, cucumbers and onion, garlic, lemon, olive oil, and mint.

Shawarma

Tender bits of skewered chicken, garlic puree, and salad wrapped in pita

Shish tawook

A chicken dish served with pure garlic paste.

Africa

Nigeria, Ethiopia, Egypt, the Democratic Republic of South Africa, Tanzania, Kenya, Algeria, Uganda, Sudan, Morocco, Ghana, Mozambique, Ivory Coast, Madagascar, Angola, Tunisia, Rwanda, Somalia, Burundi, Libya falls in Africa in the world map.

The list below is very delicious and popular snack foods in Africa
Fish rolls

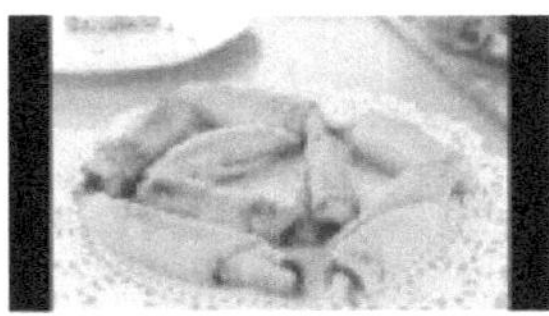

Meat Pie

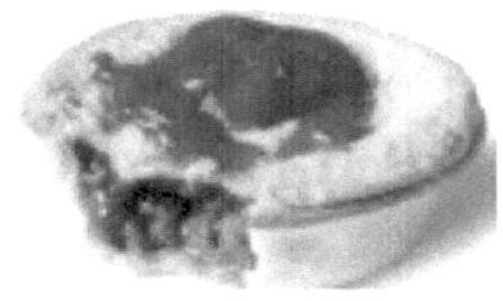

Meat fill with potato
Gateau, Nigerian Buns

Made with some flour, and vegetable oil, milk.

Fish Pie

Accra Banana

Made with cassava, banana, and salt.
Chipsimayai

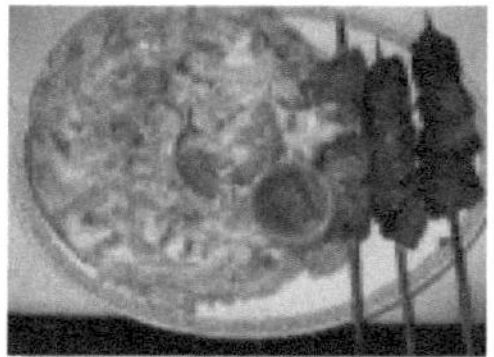

Hot chip omelets is a welcome and filling snack in Tanzania.
Kapana

Meat snack from Namibia.
Biltong

Dried pieces of meat (think jerky)

MoinMoin

Nigerian pudding made from black-eyed peas, onions, and ground pepper

Black Bean and Sweet Potato Burritos

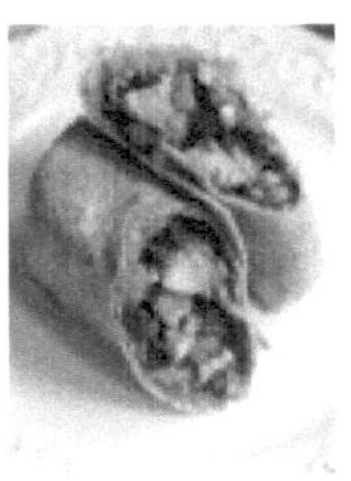

Bunny Chow

It is a hollowed-out loaf of bread or large bread roll, its cavity stuffed with everything from seafood to meat or lamb-based stews, and curries.

Back to top

CHAPTER 4

Cookies From Around the World> Most popular cookies

"A balanced diet is a cookie in each hand"
__Barbara Johnson__[1]

Most popular Cookies/biscuits From around the World

There is one more family product: a very close colleague of Snack is Cookies and a very ideal and essential part of every breakfast and when there is a need for healthy small energy filling food items.

Cookies are available across the globe in a wide range of flavors and tastes.

In this chapter, we will take you on a tour that starts from the USA to Canada through Latin America (Brazil) to Africa (South Africa), and then to Europe (Switzerland, France, Italy) from there to the UK, Middle East, Asia Pacific, and rest.

I hope you will enjoy this unique cookies journey with me and taste Cookies of each touring country.

---

1.   *https://www.azquotes.com/author/22138-Hippocrates*

Then, are you ready for this marvelous tour of Cookies excellence?

Let us start. Have a happy cookie Journey.

Before starting our journey, let us first understand what the Cookie is.

In American English, this term is used for sweet, flat, baked goods containing flour, eggs, sugar, or butter and cooking oil.

Some products contain other ingredients like raisins, oats, chocolate chips, and nuts.

Cough cookies are called biscuits in most English-speaking countries except the US and Canada. UK biscuits are cookies in the US, and vice versa, but US biscuits are called scones in the UK.

In the United Kingdom, Chewier biscuits are sometimes termed Cookies.

Let's not get confused; cookies and biscuits are synonyms; in Scotland, sometimes, plain buns are called cookies.

Sometimes cookies are named by their shape, for example, Date square, Bar, etc.

Cookies are part of snacks and beverages such as tea, coffee, or milk.

Cookies are produced at a mass scale in factories, in bakeries, or at home with variants in sandwich biscuits like custard creams, Bourbons, and Oreos, sometimes with jam filling or dipped in chocolate or with other sweetener coatings.

Factory-made cookies are sold in large malls, supermarkets, grocery shops, convenience stores, and vending machines.

GLOBAL TOUR OF COOKIES

United State of America (USA)

When we visit any shopping store or supermarket, we do find an abundant supply of cookies products whether it is healthy or not and it is not easy to choose good quality healthy cookies.

Here is the list of healthy cookies, which is widely being consumed in the US.

Kashi Chocolate Almond Butter

These cookies contain nutritious whole grains like triticale and buckwheat, Almond butter, dark chocolate chips, and crunchy almonds are the ingredients.

Snackwell's Devil's Food Cookie Cakes

These cookies are free of sketchy ingredients, but it lacks fiber and the main ingredient is sugar.

Lorna Doonehortbread Cookies

Containshigh fructose corn syrup, partially hydrogenated oils, soy lecithin, and artificial flavor.

Animal Crackers Snak-Saks

It is made up of calcium-rich sources with a grain of salt and milk. It is healthy cookies.

Walkers Shortbread Fingers

It is having four ingredients, little sugar and fat this is ready.

Newtons Fig Cookies

It is made up of real fruit, whole grains, zero trans fats, and some sugar as ingredients.

Fiber One Soft Baked Oatmeal Raisin

These cookies are soft and chewable contains some but no saturated fats.

Annie's Oatmeal Raisin

It contains organic wheat, and no HFCS or dyes it is one of the best cookies brands.

Nutter Butters

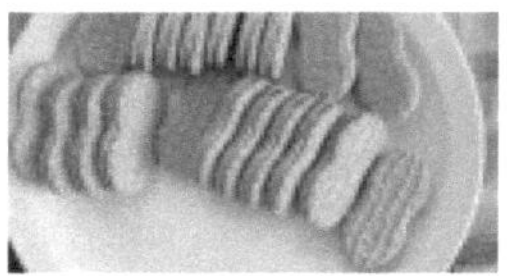

It is a peanut butter-sweet and crunchy combo. Two peanut-shaped cookies contain some saturated fats, hydrogenated oil, and soy lecithin.

Grandma's homestyle Peanut Butter Cookie

It is high-fat content cookies.

Nabisco Ginger Snaps

It is made with real molasses and ginger, sugar and salt.

Little Debbie Oatmeal Cream Pies

Cream is sandwiched between two oatmeal cookies with some artificial flavor and partially hydrogenated oil.

Oreo Golden Birthday Cake

This contains some fat and sugar.

Keebler Coconut Dreams

It contains Caramel, fudge, processed ingredients, and some sugar.

Chips Ahoy Chewy

It contains fructose corn syrup, caramel color and artificial flavor.

Chips Ahoy Chewy With Reese's

It Contains chocolate chips and peanut butter.

Pepperidge Farm Montauk Milk Chocolate

It is soft, chewy cookies made up of hydrogenated oil and saturated fat.

Latin America

After touring North America and enjoying delicious cookies, we have landed in Latin countries; let's check what they offer us; we hope it will be an altogether different experience for all of us. Let's start.

Alfajor

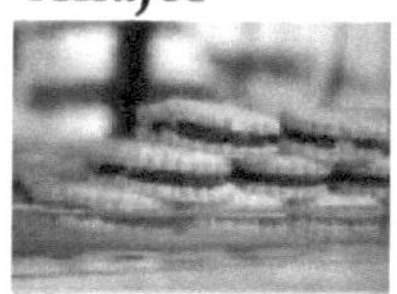

It contains dulce de Leche or milk jam stuffing sandwiched between two sweet cookies. It is then coated with chocolate or sprinkled with sugar. The name root of this cookie is from the Arabic word al-hasú, meaning stuffed.

Brigadieros Brazilian Chocolate frudge truffles

It contains caramel and chocolate flavors. Sweet condensed milk is cooked with cocoa powder until it becomes thick, then mixed with butter and vanilla and refrigerated. Then this mixture is rolled into balls and coated in chocolate sprinkles. Brigadeiros are, as per tradition, served in a small paper cup.

Cocadas

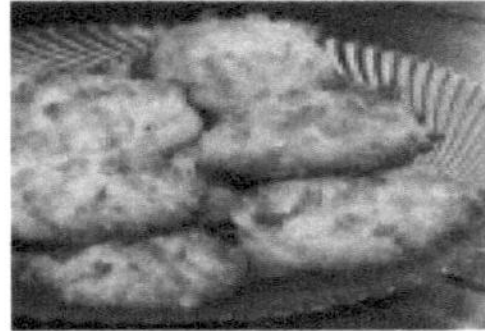

It is contains coconut macaroon decorated with dark chocolate. It has dulce de leche in the mix, providing Laticflavor. It is available in both sweet and with sweet dried coconut.

Suspiro

It is a very small sweet cookies.

Tresleches cake

It's a sponge cake drenched in a mixture of cream, condensed, and then iced with meringue or whipped cream and fresh fruit.

Tareco

Brazilian hard biscuits known as Tarecos are simple cookies consisting of wheat or corn flour, eggs, vanilla, and sugar.

Sequilhos

It is a traditional Brazilian cookie made with a combination of cornstarch, baking powder, butter, sweetened condensed milk, eggs, vanilla, and a pinch of salt; once the dough becomes stiff, it rolls into balls that are slightly flattened with a fork, giving them a decorative pattern in the process.

Africa

There was a delightful journey to Latin. The nearest place now is Africa. Would you like to taste the African variety? The answer would be yes. So go ahead and find out how to make this tour memorable; we should immediately start.

Kaakmalih

It is a savory Libyan cookie made of flour, baking powder, oil, butter, milk, and salt. The dough has two options, either braided or shaped into rings, and is dressed with sesame seeds before baking. After it is baked till golden brown, served with tea.

Krichlet

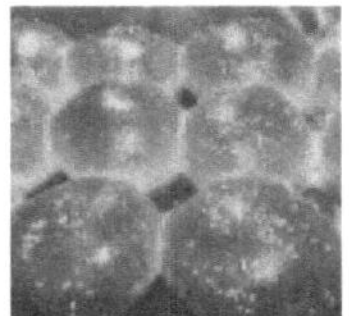

Moroccan cookies are prepared with a shortbread dough that contains aniseed, and toasted sesame seeds.

Hertzoggies

A South African cookie contains light and puff pastry tarts filled with apricot jam meringue. The crust is prepared with flour, baking powder, salt, egg yolks, sugar, butter, and nutmeg; during filling, it contains apricot jam, coconut, sugar, and beaten egg.

Cinq centimes

To make this cookie, round butter cookies are topped with a coating of peanut butter and a second layer coating of fined crushed peanuts.

Makroud

It is an Algerian cookie that contains eggs, almonds, orange flower water, and sugar. It is baled till it becomes brown and then topped with fine-grinded sugar. It is a mouth-watering experience. Isn't it?

Ghoriba

It is a Middle Eastern cookie in some variety like chewy, crumble texture, in a ball or flat shape. It consists of flour, sugar, butter, and almonds and is served with tea or coffee.

Fekkas

It is a Moroccan twice-baked cookie with a sweet and savory taste. It contains shortbread, or yeasted dough contains orange blossom water, aniseed, or citrus zest along with toasted nuts and almonds, walnuts, raisins, pistachios, or sesame seeds and served with tea or coffee.

Kaab El Ghajal

This cookie is from Morocco. It comprises a thin pastry shell wrapped with cinnamon-flavored almond enriched with orange blossom water.

Europe

Now the weather has changed from hot to cool for our taste. Europe makes up of many countries, having many varieties of cookies in this zoographical zone. There is a long list of cookies; we will review every type and comment later.

Bulgarian Maslenki

It is made with lard or butter, it is rolled out and cut into shapes and filled with rosehip, plum, or apricot jam.

Croatian Licitars

It is a honey bread cookie generally found in a heart shape but also available in other forms. It is dressed with red glaze and white icing.

Czech Vanilla crescent

It is a vanilla crescent-shaped cookies, known as anilkoverohlicky.

Lithuanian poppy seed cookies

Romania, the no-bake salam de biscuit

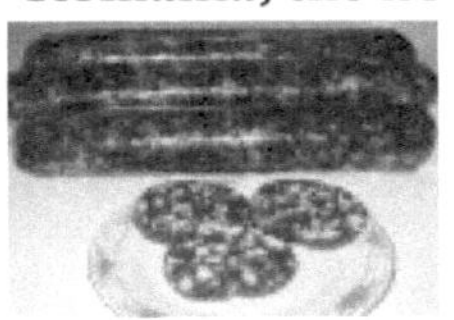

It is made up with Cocoa powder, crumbled butter cookies, walnuts, chopped Turkish delight, and sour cherries.

Russian Prvaniki

It contains sweet centers including condensed milk, chocolate, and strawberries.

Serbians Kifle

This crescent-shaped cookies made with a buttery dough and nutty filling, and kifle add a sweet-savory component. There is another variant with jam and fruit.

Polish Almond cookies

These sweet, almond-scented amaretti uses ground almonds and a pinch of cinnamon.

Polish kolaczi

This buttery cookie, which in Polish called kolaczki is made in various shapes like rounds, crescents, or diamonds. It is filled up with sweet fruits, jam and sometimes with sweet cheese mixture.

Scottish shortbread cookies

It is a buttery shortbread cookie.

Italian Biscotti

It is an almond version but available in various flavors.

French cinnamon Palmiers

It made up with a sheet of puff pastry. It can use nutmeg or pumpkin pie seasoning for a different flavor.

French vanilla sables

It is chocolate, filling with a cream cheese mixture.

Classic French Macrons

It is a crispy cookie with inside creamy.

UK

After the US, Latin, Africa, and Europe tour, we landed in the UK to get a taste of yummy cookies (Biscuits).

Let us move and see the best biscuits available here to enjoy.

In the UK, cookies are called biscuits, and Chewier biscuits in the UK are termed cookies.

We are here with a wide range of biscuits from this country.

Cookies are available in filled, bar, drop, molded, sandwich, no-bake, refrigerator, rolled, pressed, vegan, raw cookie dough, etc.

Enjoy each one with tea, coffee, or milk in our morning breakfast.

Chocolate Rounds

Shortcake biscuit, thick chocolate enjoy by dipping in a cup of tea.

Teacake

It is a Marshmallow and chocolate Biscuit.

Viennese

It is a crunchy high-quality chocolate cookie.

White Chocolate finger

Jafa cake

A spongy cookie topped with orange jelly and chocolate.

Fig roll

It is a sweet soft roll with fig paste in between.

Party Rings

This biscuit is flat in shape decorated with icing of different colors.

Wagon Wheels

It is two biscuits filled with marshmallow, jam, and dipped in chocolate.

Rich Tea Classic

It is a plain cracker.

Rocky

It is an oat biscuit covered with chocolate.

Blue Riband

Chocolate wafer cookies dipped in chocolate.

British flapjacks

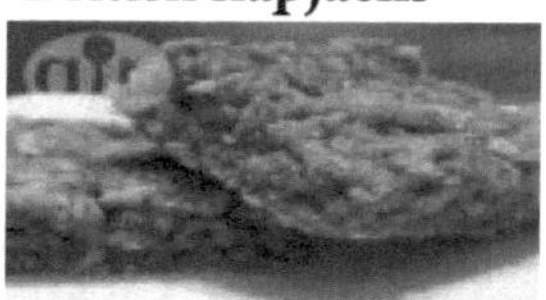

It is a bar cookie with oats, dried fruit, nuts, and golden syrup.

Chocolate Digestive

Chocolate finger

Middle East

After the UK, now it is the turn of the Middle East; I hope you will enjoy the trendy cookies of this region.

These are the top six cookies we should try before we leave the Middle East.

Ma'amul\Manena

Manena and Ma'amul are the two names of the same cookies. It's a stuffed cookie with essences of rose water and orange blossom water. It is filled with dates, almonds & pistachios.

Ghorayeba

It's made up of a shortbread recipe with almond in the center.

Baklava

Baklava is a cookie made out of layers of filo dough, butter or margarine, and chopped nuts.

Morrocan pretzels

This cookie found in both sweet or savory taste.

Kleicha

It is a stuffed with dates found in round shape and filled with cardamom or dates and coated with rose water and saffron.

Asia Pacific

We finally reached Asia and the Pacific zone to get all the remaining flavors of this big cookie market.

Macau almond cookies from China

These crumbly cookies are made up of using wooden cookie molds along with two ingredients, almonds, and mung beans.

Koloocheh from Iran

This sweet and soft Iranian cookies is round-shaped and made with plain butter and flour dough.

CinCin from Malaysia

It is made up of rice flour and a combination of red palm sugar (niham) and coconut-based melaka sugar.

Pitha from India

This popular Indian cookie is made up of rice, wheat or corn flour filled with spices, nuts, or different vegetables both in sweet and savory taste.

Silvanas from Philippines

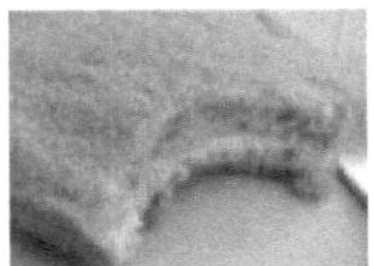

These cookie sandwiches are made with two cashew-meringue wafers within between butter-cream coated with cashew crumbs.

Non Berenji

It is a flat round shape crunchy cookies made with rice flour. It has a flavor of rose water or cardamom and finally decorated with any of poppy seeds, pistachios, barberries.

HoduGwaja

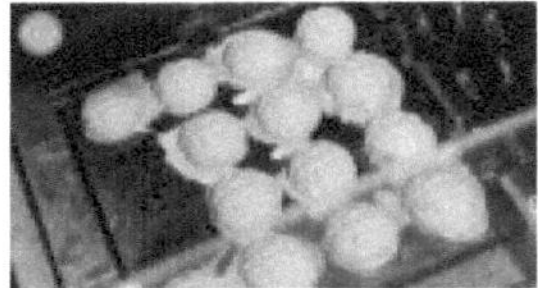

It is a south Korea cookie made with walnut and fills with pieces of walnuts and sweet red bean paste.

Tahini cookies

This crunchy sweet cookie is made with tahini sesame paste, sugar, butter, and flour. The cookie is then topped with pine nuts, sesame seeds, or almonds.

Ma'amoul

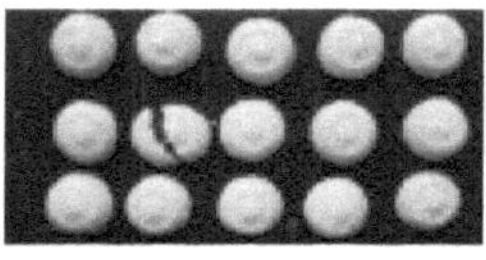

This Lebanon cookie is filled with fruits, dates, walnuts, and pistachios.

Mock Cream Donut from New Zealand

ANZAC biscuits

It Is a very popular biscuit in Australia and New Zealand army.

Afghans

This cookie is from New Zealand consists of chocolate baked with cornflakes and coated with chocolate icing and top with a walnut.

Iced VoVo from Australia

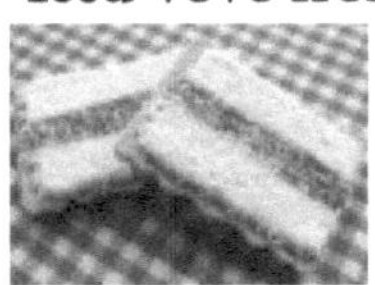

This biscuit is made from a sweet butter biscuit that is topped with raspberry jam, pink icing and coconut is sprinkled over there.

Jelly Slice from AnZ

It is a three layer biscuit made with jelly, custard and cream.

India

India is one of the largest Biscuit industry in the world.

Here are the top 10 famous biscuit brands and their popular products.

Parle

This is India's top biscuit brand. Its portfolio includes Monaco, KrackJack, Hide & Seek, Parle-G Gold, Melody chocolate,[2]Kismi Toffee Bar and Mango Bite candy.

Britannia

Portfolio of this brand contains rusk toast, bread, cake, chocolate biscuit and Good day, Marie Gold 50 50, Treat, Bourbon, and Tiger brands.

Anmol

Anmol Industries is another brand producing cakes, cookies, and biscuits in India.

Cremica

It produces healthy Mayonnaise, crackers, and cream biscuits.

Dukes

Mojo Vanilla, Kaju Delight, Cream 4 Fun Orange, Choco Desire, and Coco

---

2. http://www.walkthroughindia.com/grocery/top-12-most-popular-brands-of-chocolates-in-india/

Delight are products from Dukes.

Sunfeast

It is part of ITC limited contains many popular biscuits products like Glucose, Marie and Cream Biscuits.

Priya Gold

Priya Gold is another popular brand of India having productsPriya gold premium biscuits like mutter bite and marielite.

Oreo

This is a very popular biscuit among children.

McVitie's

This is the biscuit and cookie brand of United Biscuits.

Bisk Form

This brand is from SAJ Food products and ranked amongst the top bakery brands in India.

Patanjali

It has a wide range of products, biscuit is one of the popular product range.

Rose

Rose has a wide variety of products like Cookies, Cream Biscuits, Marie

Biscuits, Salt Biscuits, Glucose Biscuits, etc.

Back to top

CHAPTER 5

Cakes and Desserts From Around the World> Most popular cakes and deserts

"To eat is a necessity, but to eat intelligently is an art"
François de la Rochefoucauld

Most popular cakes/desserts from around the world

It is easier to imagine a birthday party with a cake or dessert. It has crossed all the barriers of ages as well as the continent.

The marriage anniversary event is among the most desirable food items after the birthday event.

Around the world, celebrating a birthday is a special event in everyone's life every year.

The way of celebration could be different, but one thing is common cutting a cake is a mandatory common global practice.

With this background, I thought to write a chapter on the range of cakes and desserts being produced and have taste around the world.

CATEGORY OF CAKES

These are broadly categorized based on ingredients and making methods.

Chocolate cake

This world's most popular and search cake having chocolate flavor.

Sponge cake

It is also known as foam cake. It has no baking powder or baking but having whipped eggs or eggs white, sugar, and flour. Air is entrapped inside beaten eggs to provide leavening.

Chiffon cake

It is the sponge cake with vegetable oil to add Moisture. It is could be in a tube pan and finally layered with fillings, and frosting.

Pound cake

It is from the same family of butter cake but named due to the ingredient's proportion in the pound. It is lightly flavored with water icing.

Genoise cake

It is the name given to spongy cake in Italy and France. Eggs are beaten in sugar till it becomes thick and flour is added and the flavor is added before final baking.

Biscuit cake

It is another form of spongy cakes but here eggs and yolks are separately whipped and then finally joined. It is lighter batter dried more than Genoise, that is why it is used in piped shape.

Angel food cake

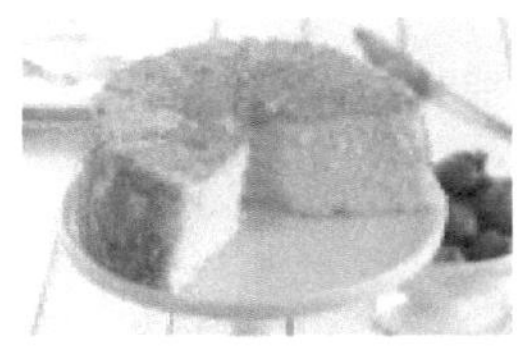

It is made from only eggs without yolk it is whipped with sugar and finally flour is added then decorated with fruits. It is a spongy caked baked in an ungreased two-piece tube pan.

Baked flourless cake

It is a baked cheesecake without flour chocolate cake. It is made in a springform pan. Often cake baking is done in a water bath.

Carrot cake

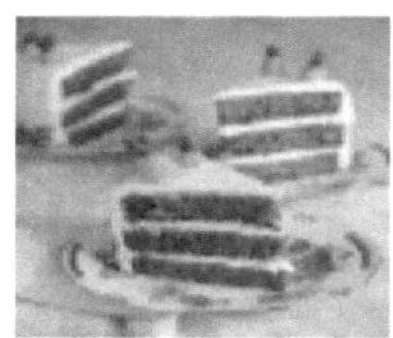

In place of butter, vegetable oil is used for making this type of cake.It is made up of whipping eggs and sugar, then the addition of oil.

Red velvet cake

Instead of butter, vegetable oil is used and cocoa added for red velvet flavor.

Butter cake

It is made from sugar, eggs, creamed butter, and flour.

Banana cake

Very popular cake throughout the world.

Lemon cake

This cake having a lemon flavor and very popular across the continent.

Ice cream cake

Another popular cake around the world.

CAKES & DESSERTS AROUND THE WORLD

United State of America (USA)

We are here with the most popular cakes from around the United States.

Salty Tart's White Chocolate Lemon Blueberry Cake

It is a Vanilla bean cake filled with lemon and blueberry which is slathered with white chocolate frosting, and finally topped with sliced lemon and berries.

Crixa's Black Forest Cake

It is a chocolate sponge cake soaked in Kirsch and stacked with whipped cream and morello cherries.

Coconut cake

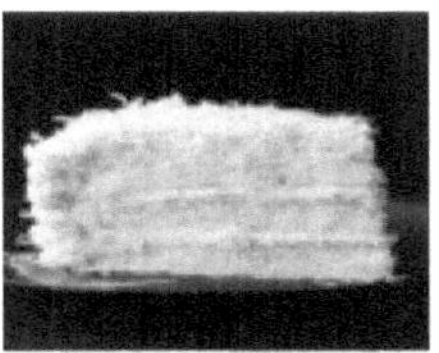

It is made from thick sponge layered with coconut flavor pastry cream. It is decorated with cheese cream frosting.

German chocolate cake

It is a combination of layers of buttermilk sponge and chocolate along with coconut and peanuts. It is decorated with pecans, desiccated coconut, or maraschino cherries.

Canada

We have seen that there is a varied range of cakes available to taste in the USA, and we have covered many of them.

On the same line, Canada also has a range of mouth-watering cakes. Would you like to have all of them? Here is the list of the most popular cakes in Canada.

Nanaimo Bar

It is a three-layer dessert made with a bottom layer of chocolate, graham cracker crumbs, nuts/coconut, a middle layer of thick custard, and a top layer topped with chocolate ganache.

Blueberry Grunt

Blueberries are slowly cooked in an open pot with water and sugar. It is topped with simple flour and butter dumplings.

PoudingChomeur

Hot caramel sauce is added to the baking pan. This sauce is soaked to the bottom during the baking process.

Beavertails

It is a deep-fried dough covered with different toppings such as Nutella, brown sugar, cinnamon, and peanut butter.

Jos Louis Cake

It is two layers of red velvet cake in between there is a cream which finally filled with chocolate.

Latin America

After visiting the US and then to Canadian cakes, now you have the turn to taste the most popular delicious cakes from Latin America.

Pastel borrach

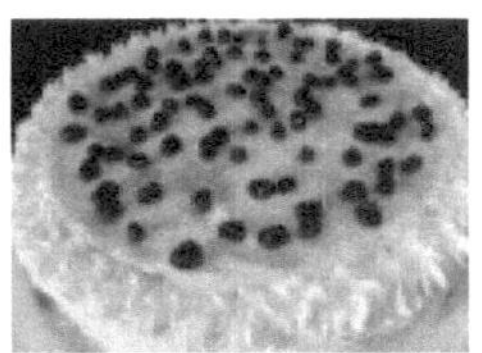

This cake contains soaking sponge cake in rum syrup. Rum syrup consists of rum, water, and sugar. This sponge cake is topped with whipped cream, egg yolks, sugar, vaporized milk, and vanilla.

Torta de Pastores

This golden brown baked cake is made from rice pudding, crumbled sponge cake, cheese, eggs, nutmeg, cinnamon, and raisins.

Milhojasdulce de leche

It is made from layers of crispy puff pastry with dulce de leche, sometimes it is coated with crème pâtissière. The final touch is given with the Italian meringue.

Tortaenvinada

This special Colombian cake is made from wine cake along with a batter of butter, flour, and eggs. Additionally, dried fruits, nuts, and caramel coloring are done and finally soaked in sweet wine for a few days.

Chajá

This cake is from Uruguay, made from sponge cake, whipped cream, peaches and, meringue. It is some times topped with dulce de leche.

Chocotorta

This Argentian cake is made from chocolate biscuits, condensed milk, and cream cheese.

Rogel

It is also an Argentian dessert consisting of thin layers of dough which are topped with a creamy dulce de leche and decorated with Italian meringue.

Chocolate santafereño

It is a Colombian dessert which is hot chocolate with cheese which is melted inside.

Canjica de Milho

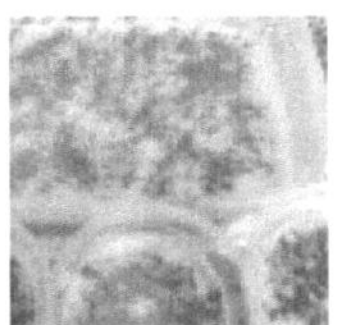

This dessert from Brazil is made from whole white maize kernels, milk, sugar, cinnamon, peanuts, and sweet condensed milk.

Chilenitos

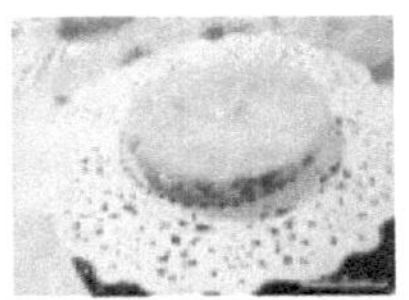

This dish is from Chile, Manjar is spread in between two flat cracker-like biscuits and finally covered with sweet meringue.

Africa

Let us see in Africa kind of cakes/desserts are there to taste and make our journey memorable.

Lemon Meringue Pie

Pie is filled with lemon curd made from lemon, starch, egg yolks, and sugar.

Queen cake: Small size

Cake is decorated with fine sugar or plain icing.

Melkkos

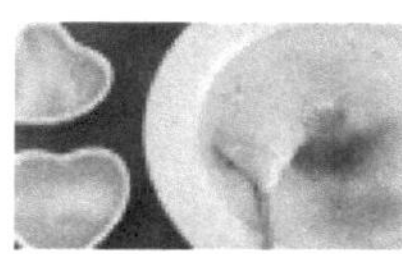

It is made from cinnamon, orange zest, butter, and naartjie.

Malva Pudding Mini Cakes

This has a spongy, caramelized texture consists of apricot jam, and served with a cream sauce topped over this.

CAKES/ DESSERT FROM EUROPE

Europe is a big continent consisting of more than 40 small countries. In this region we are an abundant range of cakes, let us check the most popular cakes from this region.

Dundee from Scotland

It is a fruitcake of cherries, candied peel, sultanas, and stuffed with almond.

Torta ricotta e pere from Italy

It is made from hazelnut sponge, ricotta cream, pear filling and syrup made from water, rum, pear brandy, and sugar.

Zagrebačkakremšnita from Croatia

This cake consists of puff pastry; above this, there is vanilla custard cream, and the top layer with chocolate.

Punschkrapfen cakes from Austria

This punch cake predominantly consists of a sponge of rum-soaked biscuits having a layer of nougat and jam. Once it is ready, topped either with cherry or chocolate.

Toucinho do céu from Portugal

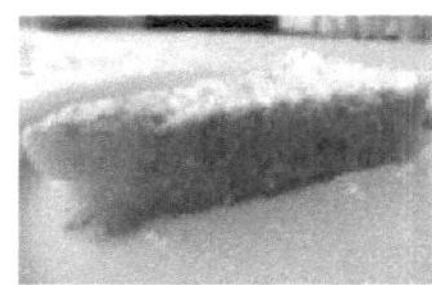

This famous cake from Portugal is made from sugary syrup, lard, almonds, egg yolks, spices, and chili squash.

TortaGurush from Bulgaria

It is made of five walnut sponges with a layer of dark chocolate. It is covered with chocolate icing and decorated with walnuts, dried coconut, and chopped almonds.

Karydopita from Greece

It is made from flour, liquor, walnuts, citrus zest, liquors, and mix of spices. It is decorated with sliced walnuts.

Kransekake from Norway

This cake is having multiple cake ring seems like a tower is made up of fined almonds, egg white, and sugar-white icing.

Mona de Pasqua from Spain

This cake is a combination of sweet brioche dough, stuffed with candied fruit and finally topping of boiled eggs.

Boterkoek from Netherland

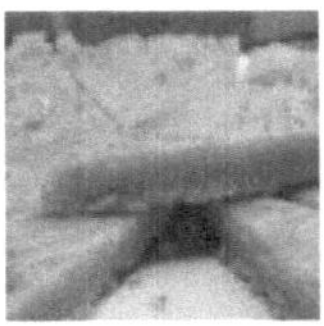

This is an old traditional cake consists of flour, butter, sugar, eggs, and vanilla. To add flavor lemon zest may be used.

Ateau Basque cake from France

This is made from layers of shortcrust pastry and filled with black cherry preserve.

Binenstich Germany

In between two layers of yeasted pastry dough cream is filled and finally decorated with honey and almond.

Sękacz from Poland

This cake making process is different. In this process batter layer is spread on a moving horizontal split, simultaneously bales in over.

Amandine from Romania

It is a traditional Romanian cake made from sponge cake (a combination of eggs, water, flour, sugar, oil, and cocoa), the syrup (consists of sugar, water, and rum, the filling (consists of butter, vanilla, cocoa, and sugar)and the glazing is made with whipping cream, and chocolate.

Prinsesstarta from Sweden

It is a spongy layer cake coated with vanilla buttercream and finally topped with whipped cream and marzipan.

Smetannik from Rusia

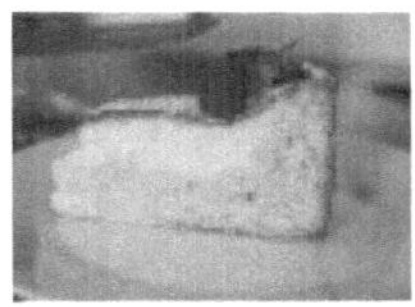

This cake is consisting of sugar, eggs, honey, flour, and ream fasting of sour cream, cream cheese, milk, and vanilla.

Lagkage from Denmark

Three layers of the sponge are filled with fresh fruit and pastry creams.

Kremnarezina from Slovenia

This Slovenian cake is made from cream cake with a golden, crispy pastry, topped with vanilla and whipped cream, and finally decorated with icing sugar.

SomlóiGaluska from Hungary

This cake is the combination of sponge, and custard cream, raisins drenched in rum and finally topped with whipped cream.

Bublanina from the Czech republic

It is the composition of sponge cake, eggs, butter, sugar, flour, and various fruits, for example, cherries, strawberries, blueberries, and apricots.

CAKES/ DESSERTS FROM UK

We have shared cakes and desserts from around the world and briefly explained cakes and desserts from the UK. In the UK, a wide range is available, and no one can leave without tasting these.

Coffee and Walnut Cake

This cake has two pastry layers with coffee-flavored butter icing in between these.

Fruit Cake

It consists of dried fruits, and nuts are soaked in the sugar.

Collin the Caterpillar Cake

It is a combination of milk chocolate beans that are rich sugar-coated.

Carrot Cake

The main ingredients are carrot pineapple, raisins, nuts, and it is glazed with cream cheese frosting coating.

Chelsea cake

Thedough is flavored with cinnamon, mixed spice, and lemon peel.

Queen Elizabeth Cakes

This cake is made from date nut cake that is topped with icing with shredded coconut.

Banbury Cakes

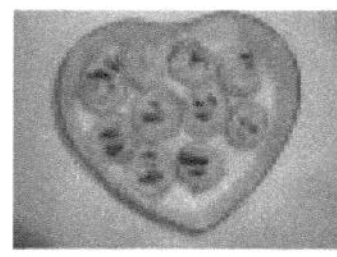

It is a spiced, currant-filled flat pastry cake.

Simnel

It is made with flour, eggs, sugar, milk, and flour then batter is mixed with dried fruit for example currants.

Madeira

It is a popular tea time sponge cake sprayed with icing sugar, and topped with candied orange peel.

Battenberg

It is a colored genoisesponge topped with apricot jam, and almond paste.

Victoria sponge

This sponge cake is filled with strawberry jam, or with apricot, and greengage jam.

Crumpet

It is a small round pancake that is made up of flour, yeast, sugar, salt, milk, baking powder or baking soda.

CAKES/ DESSERTS FROM ASIA PACIFIC

In this zone, a large part of the world's population is living, so having a wide range of cakes/dessert is enjoyed by millions of people.

India

Chocolate cakes

This is one of the most popular chocolate cake in the country.
Vanilla cake

This is another popular birthday cake after chocolate cake in India.
Pineapple cakes

This is one of party favorite cake.
Black forest cakes

This is the combination of layers of chocolate joined with whipped cream, and top decorated with red cherries.
Butterscotch cake

Coffee Cake

This is a perfect coffee lover dessert.

Banana cake

It is a moist texture and strong flavor.

Lemon cake

It is also one of the favorite lemon flavor cake

Red velvet cake

This is a high cocoa stuffed cake.

China

Sticky Rice Cakes (Lean go niangao)

This Chinese new year cake is made from glutinous rice, and brown sugar.

Water Chestnut Cake

This cake is made from shredded Chinese water chestnut and cuts into small squares.

Eight Treasure Rice (babaofan)

Dessert is the combination of glutinous rice, and a variety of dried fruits and nuts along with red dates, and lotus seeds.

Mooncakes

This sweet is made of nuts, fruits, red bean paste, and lotus seeds paste.
Double-skin Milk

Dessert is consists of milk, egg white, and sugar.
Green Bean Cake

This specialty delicious cake is made from green beans.
Deep-fried mántou

It is a deep-fried bun served with condensed milk.
Japan
Wakakusa

This is a green-tinted sugar and rice powder-covered rectangular rice cake.
Kurumi mocha

It is made from mochi (sticky rice cake), and cream of walnut sauce.

Habutae mocha

This is also one of the cake quality popular dessert made from rice flour, syrup, and sugar.

Imagawayaki

This is a sponge cake filled up with red bean mixture, and fried in the pan with egg-based batter.

Mushi pan

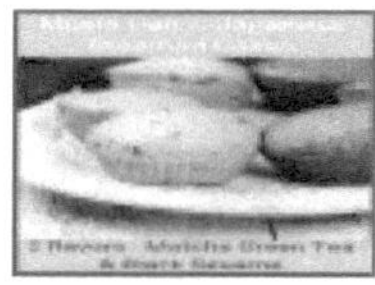

Steamed bun is prepared with flour, baking powder, eggs, and sugar.

Hishi mocha

This is a glutinous mochi base having three layers pink layer of jasmine flavor, middle white layer of water chestnuts, and last layer green layer of mugwort.

Uiro

Cake is steamed for its chewing texture made from rice flour, sugar, and water.

Sakura mocha

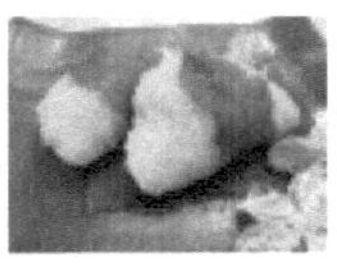

This famous dessert that is made from sakura (i.e. cherry blossom), pink color containing red bean paste.

Australia

This country has its product range which they offer to us to taste each of them.

Tasmanian apple cake

It is a combination of a batter of flour, butter, baking powder eggs, and sugar along with chopped apples, cinnamon, zest, and lemon juice.

Lamington

The dough that is drenched in chocolate, and finally dusted with fined dried coconut.

Pavlova

This dessert is consists of snowy meringue, and varieties of fruits.

Red velvet cake

This is one of the very popular cakes in the country.

Neapolitan Cake with Frosting Rosettes

This is one of the most popular birthday cake.
Buttercake with lemon icing

This is a yogurt and lemon drizzle cake.
Fruit cake

It is a fruit-based cake.
Black forest cake

One of the most popular cakes in the world.

New Zealand

Cameo Cream
Coconut taster cream is kept in between two chocolate biscuits.
Pineapple Lumps

It is made with a chocolate coating over chewy pineapple.
Lolly cake

The cake combines crushed biscuits, butter, condensed milk, and marshmallow topped with shredded coconut.
Jelly slice

This dessert is very colorful, with a base of cookies and topped with creamy custard. The custard is made of condensed milk and lemon, and the dessert top consists of jelly or fruit jam.
Hokey pokey ice cream

It is vanilla-flavored ice cream, and crumbled honeycomb toffee is sprinkled all over there.

Pavlova

This dessert is consists of snowy meringue, and varieties of fruits.
Banana cake

This is one of the most search cakes in the country.
Red velvet cake

This is another very popular cake of the country although it is liked globally.
Thailand
Custard-Filled Bread

This is a very popular dessert of Thailand liked by most of the tourists made from bun that is topped with chocolate syrup.

Thai-Style Crème Caramel

This mouth-watering coconut dessert is made from coconut milk.

Banana Leaf And Sticky Rice

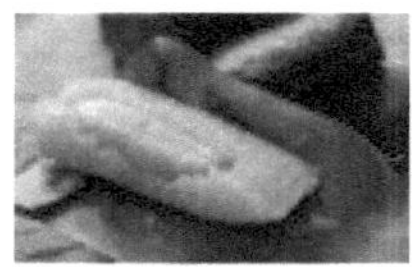

This vegan dish is made using black beans, coconut milk, sugar, and sticky rice.

Thai Mango Sticky Rice – KhaoNiaoMamuang

This unique dessert is made from sliced mangoes, sticky rice, and coconut milk poured on them and sprinkled with fried mung beans.

Thai Crispy Pancakes – KhanomBuang

This pancake is made from rice, mung bean flour, and coconut cream is topped over there.

Thai Sweet Rolled Sesame Pancakes – TuangMuan Sot

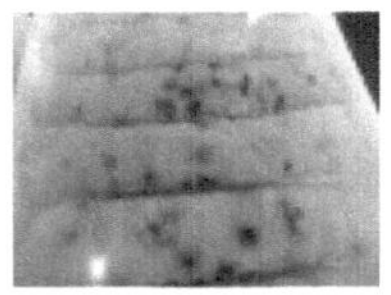

This sesame seeds pancake is flavored with coconut, corn, and taro.

Black Sesame Dumplings in Ginger Soup – Bua Loy Nam King

This dessert is consisting of round dumplings of rice flour that are filled with black sesame paste.

Indonesia

Wingko

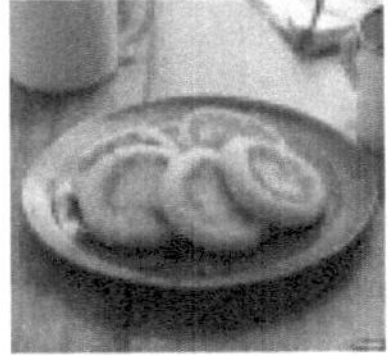

This cake is based on rice flour, grated coconut, and fresh coconut milk.

Kueputu

Steamed cake is made from rice flour, grated coconut, and fresh coconut milk.

Variations of Kue Lapis Legit

This consists of two layers, one in a lighter shade and another one in a darker shade of cocoa.

GetukLindri cake

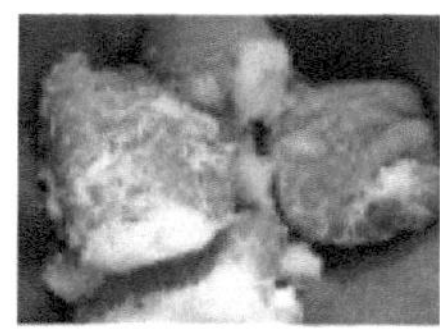

This cake is made with peeled cassava mixed with vanilla, salt, and coconut.

Lumpur Cake

The cake consists of potato and egg, finally topped with raisin.

Back to top

CHAPTER 6

Pizzas From Around the World> Most popular pizzas

"If you really want to make a friend, go to someone's house and eat with him, the people who give you their food, give their heart"
Cesar Chavez

Most popular pizzas from around the world

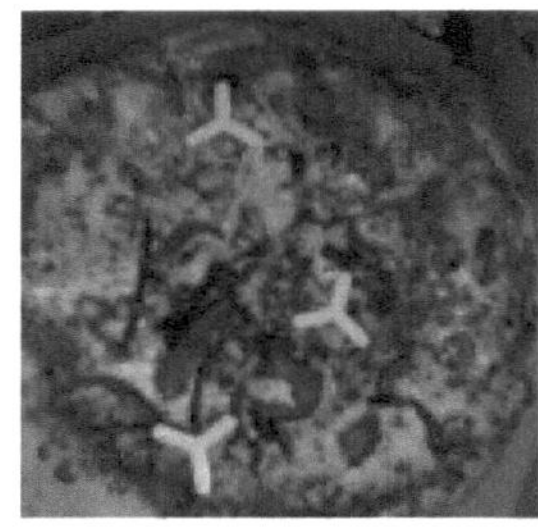

The word pizza is thought to be derived from the Latin word pinsa, which means a flatbread. It is an Italian-origin dish prepared with bread, tomato, and other ingredients, which are served with cheese.

Let us start our well-known global pizza journey, but this time we will begin with international pizza brands at a glance summary of them.

MOST POPULAR PIZZA BRAND

A tasty pizza is everyone's love across the world. Top Pizza brand has a large pizza chain across the globe.

The big brand has opened its outlet almost in every big town with committed timely delivery of their product to serve the customer better at their doorstep.

Now let us see the list of the world's top 10 largest pizza chains.

This list is prepared based on their market share, product uniqueness, and other customer delights factors.

Domino's Pizza

It is the world's no.1 pizza company with a delivery commitment of 30 minutes else free pizza. It is the USP of this brand, apart from outstanding product quality and services.

Pizza hut

It is the second most pizza company in the world. This food chain set itself in pan pizza and stuffed crusts.

Little Caesars

The popularity of this pizza chain is increased exponentially in the United state, and it is appreciated as being the fastest-growing pizza chain.

Papa John's

This is the pizza chain that had offered online ordering. They also claim for using only fresh ingredients.

California Pizza Kitchen

This brand is known for California-style pies and spiced pizza with some invention and nontraditional topping.

Papa Murphy's

This famous brand has a taking-and-bake strategy; people can conveniently take raw pizza and bake it.

Sbarro: This pizza restaurant usually is founded at the shopping mall only.

Marco's Pizza

It is America's one of the fastest-growing pizza chains. The USP of this chain is generous portions, and fresh ingredients are sliced, chopped, and prepared in their kitchen.

Peter Piper Pizza

They peter piper pizza maintains a similarly kid-friendly, festive environment, often featuring game rooms with arcades, and even playground equipment.

CiCi's Pizza

This pizza chain is quite popular for its pizza bar.

MOST POPULAR PIZZA OF THE WORLD

Primo from Portugal

This tasty pizza base is beautifully topped with different ingredients, and vegetables.

Pizzarium pizza from Italy

This delicious Italian pizza is very soft, and top of this is covered with tasty Italian ingredients.

Pizza palaRomana from Thailand

Beauty of this pizza is that it is made up of mostly imported ingredients.

Hank Pizza from France

This is purely a vegan pizza, its topping is based on the plant-based ingredients.

Fooccaceria Toscana from Spain

This thick base pizza is made up of fresh topping, and a lot of cheese.
Sicilia's from Saudi Arabia

This is a very soft mouthwatering pizza that has a thick base with topping from imported ingredients.
Galleria Umberto from USA

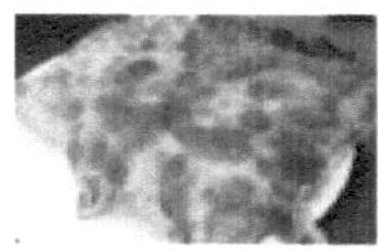

It is a thick crunchy base loaded with a lot of cheese.
Nolita from Philippines

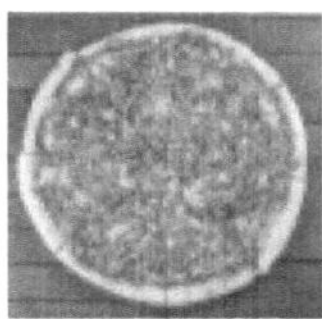

It is a combination of a thin crust with cheese, and a lot of tomato sauce.
Pizza Tirolese from Italy

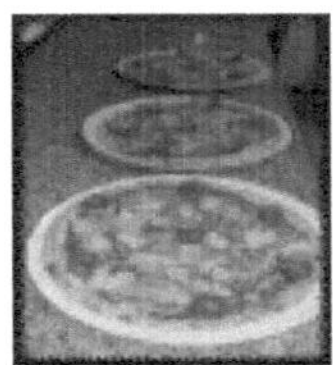

This delicious pizza is made up of thin slices of tirolek speck, mozzarella, and tomato.

Garlic fingers from Canada

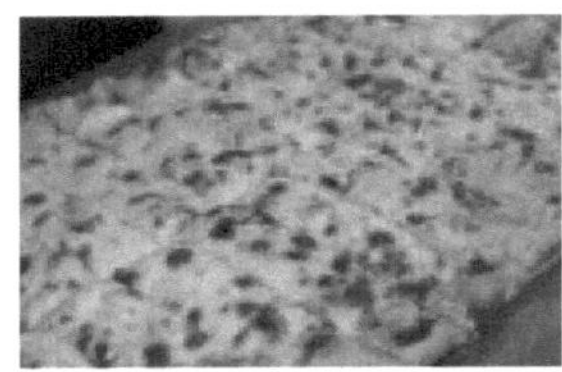

Dough base is consists of garlic butter, cheese, parsley, dill, and vegetables.

St. Louis-style pizza from USA

It is made up of provel, white cheddar (i.e. cheese), swiss cheese, and cheese made with provolone (an Italian soft smoked cheese).

Pizza Grandiosa from Norway

This first frozen pizza from Norway is made with pizza meat, tomato sauce, pepper, and Jarlsberg.

Pizza Rustika from Italy

This is three-layer pizza with extreme two layers are of crust and in between these two there is a hum, prosciutto, Italian cheese, salami, and eggs.

Fugazzeta from Argentina

This Argentian pizza is made up of mozzarella-stuffed and topped with onions.

Pizza e fichi from Italy

This delicious Bianca pizza combines garlic, olive oil, mozzarella salt, and seldom rosemary leaves.

Tomato pie from USA

Thick and crispy crust is added with cheese, and tomato pie.

Greek Pizza from USA

This Greek-style pizza is made up of wettish dough, tomato sauce, greasy cheese, and oregano.

Pizza ai fungi from Italy

This delicious traditional Italian pizza is made with mushrooms, parsley, oil, tomato sauce, and mozzarella cheese.

Hawaiian pizza from Canada

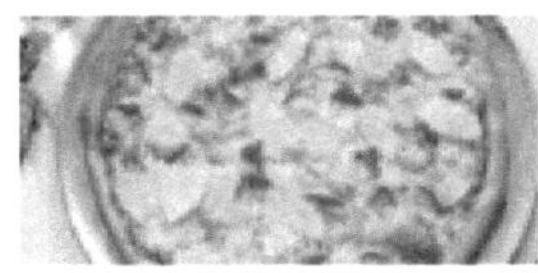

It is topped with topped ham, cheese, and pineapple slice.

Pizza vegitariana from Italy

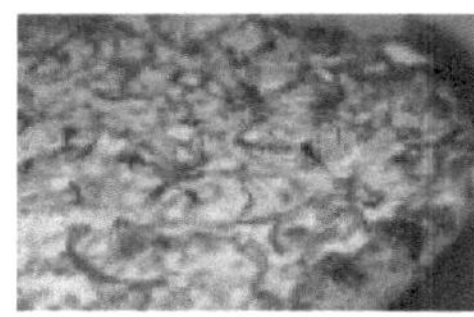

It is consisting of dough, tomato sauce, mozzarella, fresh vegetables, eggplants, and peppers.

Pizza cake from Canada

This pizza has multiple layers but basic ingredients are the same as tomato sauce, pepperoni, and cheese.

Grandma pie from USA

It is topped with grated mozzarella, garlic, tomato sauce, and olive oil, additionally sausages, and broccoli rabe can be added.

Indian Pizza

In India, Italian pizza is very popular but there has been a moderation in the topping by using unique ingredients like Tandoori chicken and Paneer.

Sfincione pizza from Italy

It is a thick, spongy crust that is topped with bread crumbs, caciocavallo, and onions.

Zapiekanka from Poland

It Is like an open sandwich topped with mushroom, cheese, polish ketchup, and feta cheese.

Margherita pizza from Italy

It is also popularly known as Neapolitan pizza, the baked pie is topped with a sauce made from mozzarella, basil, garlic, Marzano tomatoes, and olive oil.

Lahmacun or Lahmajoun from Turkey

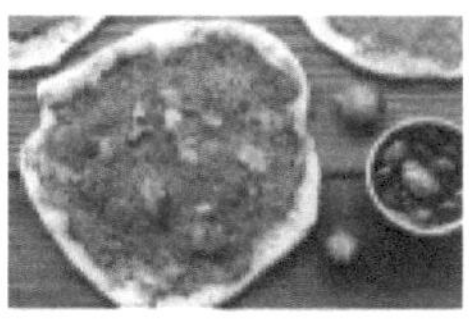

Turkish bread is topped with minced meat, tomato, lettuce, lemon, parsley, and onion.

Okonomiyaki from Japan

Okonomiyaki cake is consisting of cabbage, seafood, and savory sauces like an octopus, yam, and shrimp.

Pissaladiere from France

This salty cake is consisting of onion, herbs, and anchovies.

Coca from Spain

This Spanish pizza is topped with anchovies, olive oil, pine nuts, spinach, citrus rind, and mushrooms.

Manakish from Lebanon

Pie includes thyme, oregano, cheese, meat, and sesame seeds.

Bulgogi pizza from Korea

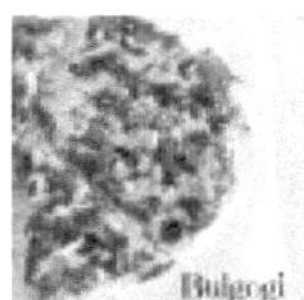

Pie is added with bulgogi (Korean barbecued beef), corn, peppers, and bulgogi sauce.

Lángos from Hungary

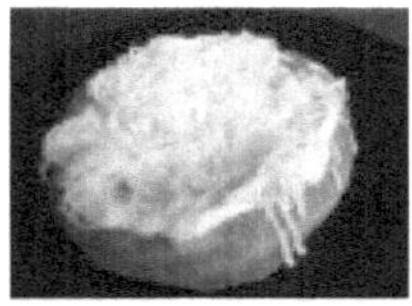

Bread is made with sour cream or yogurt, added with shredded cheese, and garlic.

Banana pizza from Iceland

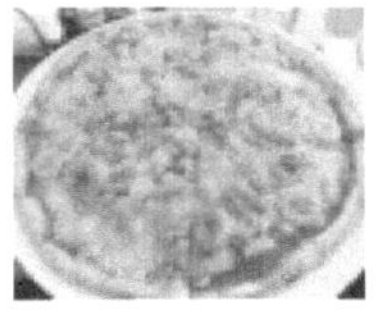

Here pizza is topped with banana and sometimes with pineapple.

Flammkuchen from Germany

It is a thin and crispy pizza that is added with bacon, caramelized onion, and crème fraîche.

Sfiha from Lebnan and Brazil

It is a round pie that is topped with ground mutton, cheese, and vegetables.

Back to top

CHAPTER 7

Most Popular Foods From Around the World> Most popular foods

"Cooking is all about people. Food is maybe the only universal thing that really has the power to bring everyone together. No matter what culture, everywhere around the world, people eat together."
Guy Fieri

In every country, even in a country with different geographical locations, foods choice, and tastes are other; this might be due to the surrounding climatic condition, which is suitable for growing specific kinds of food products and its abundant availability in that area and people living there, are used to with this particular kind of food products, and that becomes the first choice of their daily meal.

In this chapter, we have once again come up with a wide range of food products being eaten across the globe daily by billions of people.

We are covering once again continent-wise food habits of the people, so when you visit this continent never miss to have a taste of them, because this would be a lifetime experience for them, as it would not be possible to take a whole world tour by everyone, but when they visit any specific country, should have a list of products. Importantly, it should be noticed.

CATEGORY OF FOODS

- Foods are broadly categorized as under:
- Dairy Products
- Fats & oils
- Fruits and vegetables
- Confectionery
- Cereal & cereal products
- Bakery products
- Meat & Poultry and its products
- Fish & fish products
- Egg and egg products
- Sweeteners
- Salt, spices, sauces, soup, salads and protein products
- Foodstuff intended for nutritional requirement fulfillment
- Beverages Ready to Eat products.

GLOBAL TOUR OF FOOD
United State of America (USA)

When you are in America, there is an unlimited range of food products available here; selecting the best one will always be a challenge. Hence we are here with a list of some popular food from all across the states of this country.

The United state is a multicultural country; there are people from all part of the world who lives together, so there is cultural diversity; the same is reflected in food also, here you can find a wide product range.

We are sharing the most popular foods in this country.

Pot roast

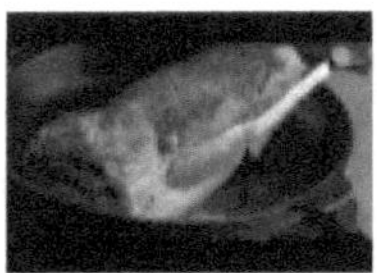

It is a meat deeply roasted with carrot, onion and potato.

Jerky

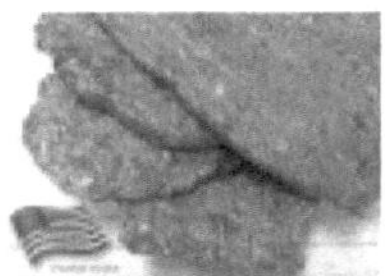

It is a high protein content dehydrated meat.

Jambalaya

It is made with meat, vegetable, rice along with tomato and cajun.

Biscuit and gravy

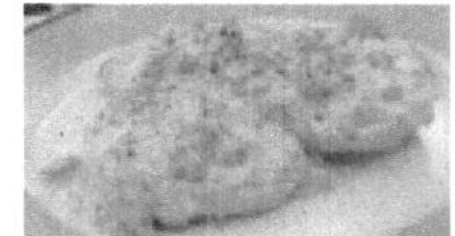

It is made up of biscuit, meat sausage, meat, and black pepper gravy.
Chicken fried steak

Chicken fried steam came in combination with potato and black peas.
Wild Alaska salmon

This non-farming fish is prepared with mustard or real maple syrup.
Meatloaf

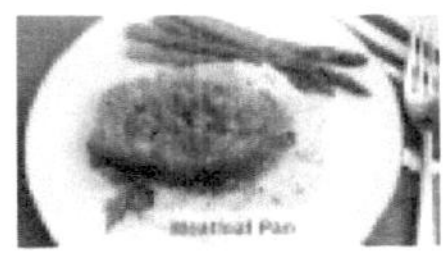

This is made up with a topping of slices of salt meat laid and a dish to be served with brown mushroom sauce.
Cioppino

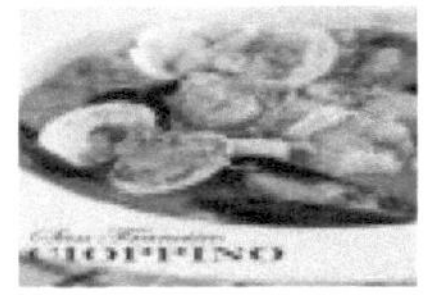

This dish is produced when chopped fish is cooked with tomato gravy along with wine and spice.

Fried chicken and waffles

This fried chicken is eaten with popcorn, finger or bites.

New Mexican flat enchiladas

It is a Mexican fish & meat product served with red chili sauce.

Buffalo wings

It is a hot and spicy buffalo wings.

Indian Frybread

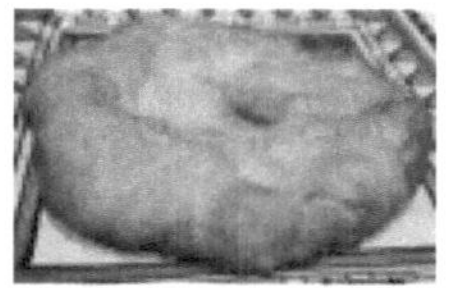

It is a high-calorie food consists of meat, onion, cheese, and vegetable leaves.

Barbecue ribs

It is a smoked meat food product.

Blueberry Cobbler

It is in combination with crust, dough, or batter.

Clam Chowder

Recipe for this dish is mixing shellfish with meat which is salted , cream and herbs.

Texas Barbecue

It is a mesquite smoked meat product from Texas.
Tacos

Chicken is stuffed in fried Taquitos.
Hot dog

Macaroni and cheese

Fried green tomato

This is a vegan dish of fried green tomato.
Chimichangas

It is a deep-fried burrito.
Hot Brown

In consists of Turkey, tomato, bacon and mix with Mornaysauce. (This sauce is made from bechamel sauce along with shredded cheese).
Shrimp Gumbo

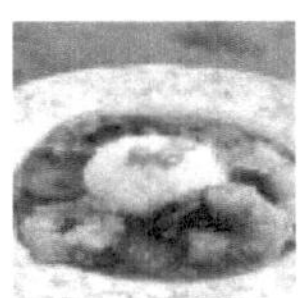

Recipe for this food is a combination of roux, sausage, okra, pepper, and shellfish.
Cold lobster Roll

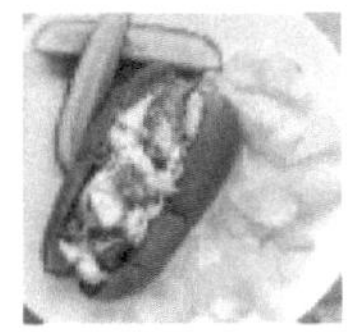

Wild Rice Soup

Fried Okra

Chislic

It is made of mutton, lamb, which is mixed with garlic and salt, finally grilled or deep-fried.

Nashville Hot Chicken

It is a chicken that is served with a paste of lard and cayenne pepper.

Canada

Canadian has a different range of foods that are very popular there. Herewith please find all Canadian foods for your ready reference when you are here.

Caesar

This is roasted, It is made from vegetable, hot dog, meat, cheeseburger, and chicken.

Butter Tarts

Recipe is crumbled crust with cream of butter, egg, and sugar.

Split Pea Soup

It is a combination of cured meats and dried peas.

Tourtière

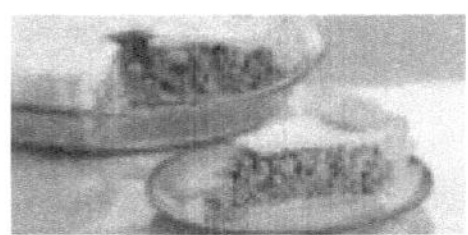

It is made with meat, veal along with herbs, and spice.

SASKATOON BERRY PIE

It has a sweet and almond taste.

Poutine

Consist of Fries, cheese curd, along with meat, bacon, and smoked meat.

PEAMEAL BACON

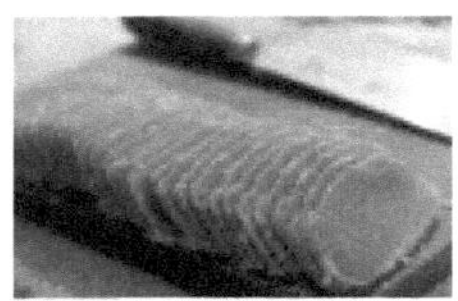

It is a boneless meat loin rolled with cornmeal.

Chicken Fricot

It is a meat stew cooked with potatoes, onions,other vegetables, and dumplings.

Rappie Pie

It is a potato dish made with meat broth, onions, and chicken.
Cretons Quebec pate

It made up of meat, onions, and spices.
Montreal Smoked Meat

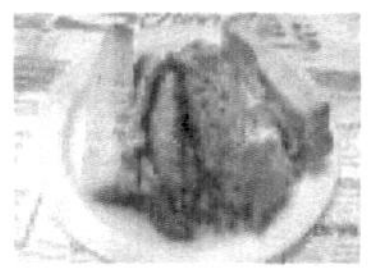

It is salted smoked meat.
Montreal style bagels

This sweet dish is made from boiling Bagels sweetener and honey.
Great Lakes Perch

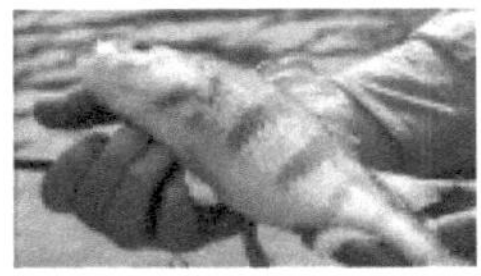

This dish is a little sweeter. It is fish from the lake made with thin white meat.

Hodge Podge

It is a vegetable dish made from potatoes, fresh peas, green beans, wax beans, carrots along with pepper, butter, and salt.

Latin America

After going through US and Canadian food, it is time to have a flavor of a wide range of Latin foods.

Salvadoran Pupusas

It is filled with cheese, refried beans, and seasoned meat along with platanos.

Dominican mangú

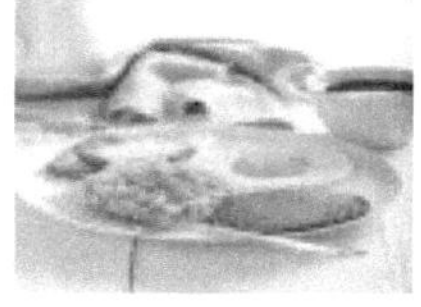

It is made from fried salami, eggs, avacado, questofrito along with plantains, and onion.

Ropavieja

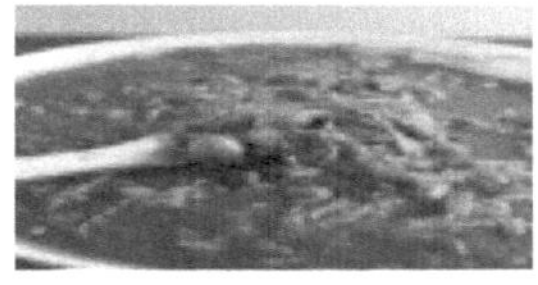

It is savory stewed meat layered over piping-hot, butter mixed white rice, and black beans.

Peruvian ceviche

It is a fish product get dipped in lime, onions, suca, and peppers

Arepa

It is a white dough made from corn flour and filled with cheese, avocado, and, beans or meat.

Tamales

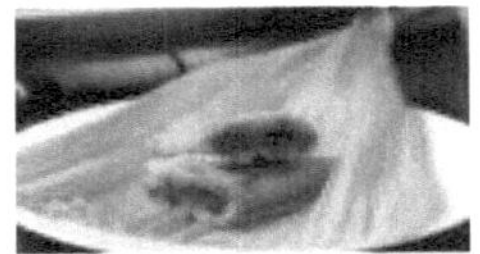

Tamales dough is prepared from corn, then it is filled with meat or chicken, wrapped in banana leaf, and finally steamed and served.

Tacos

Corn / Wheat tortilla is filled with meat, chicken, seafood, vegetables, and cheese.

Cuban Sandwich

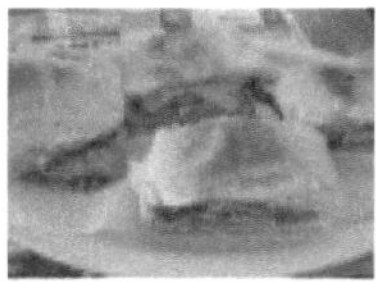

It is prepared from Cuban bread, ham, pickles, cheese, and roast meat.

EmpanadasArgentinas

Empanadas is made from folded dough stuffed with meat, cheese, and vegetables.

Africa

When we visit Latin and leave without a visit to Africa, it would not be justice, which means Africa have their range of African foods and taste, and anyone visiting can only leave with this. See what African foods are here that should be tried.

Pap envleis/Shisanyama from South Africa

It is a combination of Barbecued meat and maize porridge served with spicy gravy.

Piripiri chicken from Mozambique

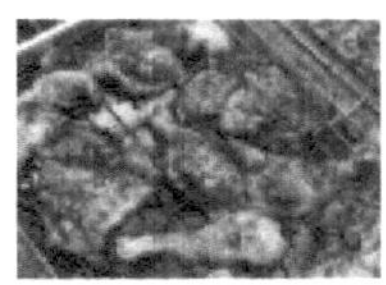

This dish consists of chicken with lime, pepper, garlic, coconut milk along with piripiri sauce.

Jollof rice and egusi soup from Nigeria

Rice, tomatoes, onions and pepper is served along with egusi soup.

Bunny chow from South Africa

It made up of a loaf white bread filled with meat and vegetable hot curry.

Kapenta with sadza from Zimbabwe

This African dish is made from Kapenta and maize porridge which is called sadza, tomatoes, onions, and groundnut powder.

Chambo with nsima from Malawi

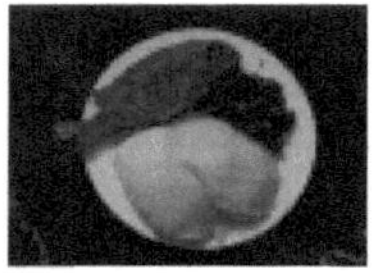

It is a fish along with nasima (maize porridge), pumpkin or cassava leaves, tomatoes, and groundnut powder.

Muamba de Galinha from Angola

It is known as chicken muamba, and along with chicken it consists of palm oil, garlic, chili, and okra.

Cape breyani from South Africa

It very good flavor food dish made with marinated meat, rice, lentils and spice and added with fried onion and boiled egg.

Koshari from Egypt

It is a dish of rice, lentils, macaroni, garlic and chickpeas mixed with sharp chili spicy tomato sauce, and covering fried onion.

Chicken Kebabs from Egypt

It is a boneless chicken breasts and made spicy by using cardamom and black pepper.

Pastillaaupigeon/b'stilla from Morocco

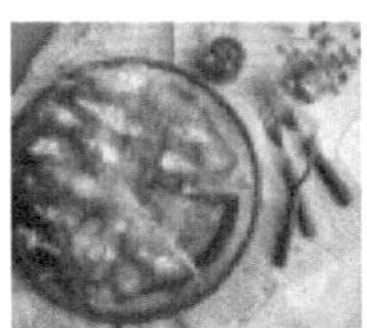

It is a another chicken item becomes thicker with a sauce of egg, pastry, and spice.

Nyamanairio from Kenya

This popular spicy roasted meat dish from Kenya made from mashed potato, bean, peas, onion, and corn.

Europe

Food availability and selection varied as per the climatic conditions. European countries have different food choices as well as varieties.

Europe is a big continent comprised of 40+ countries connected geographically and with food culture.

Here are the food products from all around Europe.

Arancini from Italy

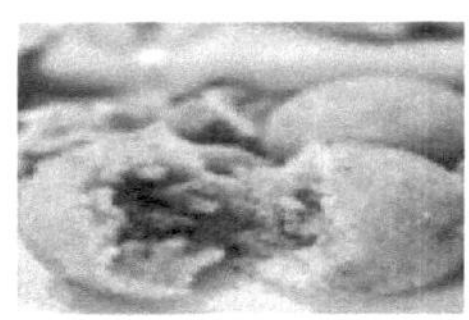

It is a dish made from meat, tomato, mushrooms, pistachios, and mozzarella is stuffed in a fried rice ball.

Pierogi from Poland

Potatoes, ground meat, sauerkraut, cheese, or fruit is filled in the dumpling and over the top, there is fried onion, sour cream, and butter.

Palatschinken from Austria

It is a crepe served along with apricot jam, cream or nutella.

Currywurst from Germany

It is a fried meat sausage served with curry ketchup and french fries.

Potica from Slovenia

This dish is made from rolled sweet dough with a paste of ground nuts & honey.

Moussaka from Greece

It is made from ground meat and tomato or béchamel sauce layer over potato or some time with sweet & tendered vegetables.

Köttbullar from Sweden

This consists of cream and breadcrumbs soaked in milk and serve with gravy, boiled potatoes and lingonberry jam.

Palacinky from Czech

This Czech dish is consisting of dough crepe which is served with plum jam, strawberry, and apricot.

Doner Kebab from Italy

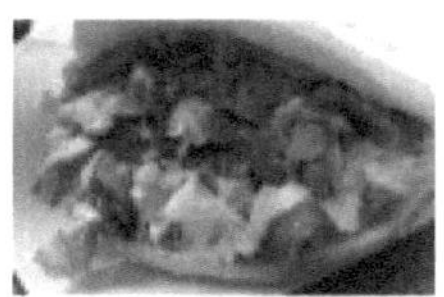

It is a combination of bread and meat served with lettuce, tomato, and olives.

Goulash

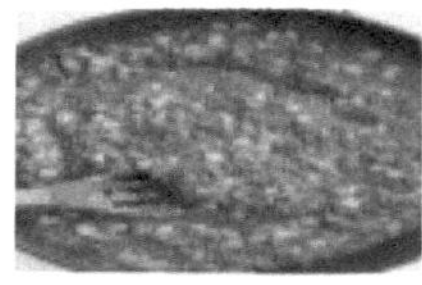

It consists of vegetables and meat that is seasoned with salt, herb,spices and pepper and served with bread, and beverage.

Crème Catalan from Spain

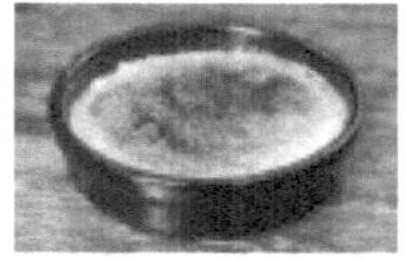

It is a custard dish with brownish caramel.
Struklji from Slovenia

These cheese pancakes are made with tarragon.
Herring from Netherland

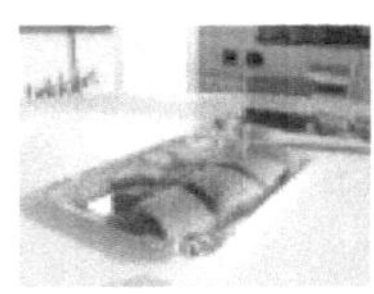

It is a popular silverfish food.
Eisbein from Germany

It is a boiled meat knuckle, sauerkraut and mustard with a drink.
Moules-frites from Belgium

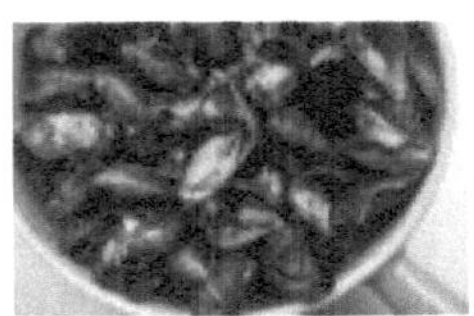

It is a Moules-frites cooked in white wine, cream and with fries.

Faves a la Catalana from Spain

This dish is consisting of butifarranegra, sausages, garlic, fava beans, pancetta along with spices and herbs.

UK

You are now enjoying this food global tour with all variances from different countries and would be amazed to know that so much wide range is available from one part of the world to another part of the world.

The UK is our other destination with its range of food products. Let us travel all.

English Breakfast

It is a combination of bacon, sausages, tomato, mushroom, egg along with tea, and toast.

Meat Pie

Made from meat meat, pastry crust, and gelatin.

Haggis

It is consisting of sheep's organs, oatmeal, onion, suet, and seasoning ingredients.

Fish and chips

Bangers and Mash

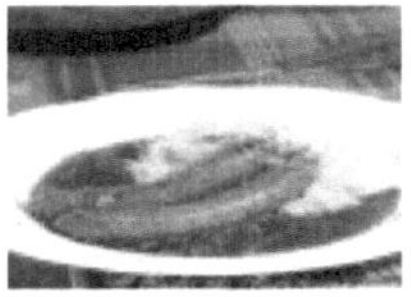

It is a Sausages and Mashed potatoes food item.

Sunday Roast

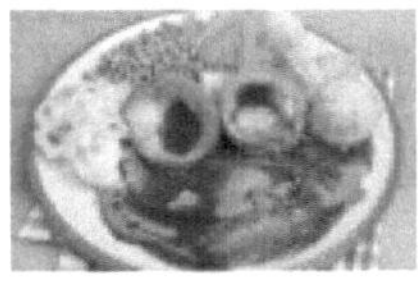

This food is made from chicken and lamb roast.

Welsh Cawl

It consisting of meat, carrots, leek, and potatoes.
Cornish Pasty

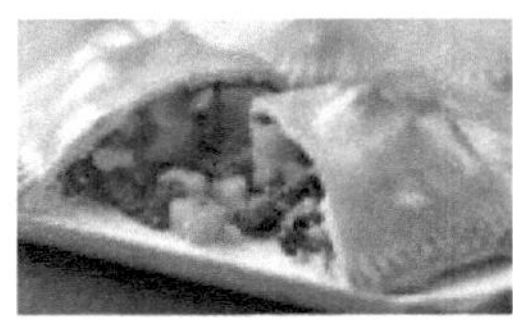

Baked pastry is filled with meat, potato, onion, and swede.
Chips and Gravy

It is a gravy fish and chips food item.
Lancashire hotpot

This special dish is made from a combination of mutton or lamb and vegetables, and sliced potatoes.
Chicken tikka masala

Roasted chicken served with spicy sauce.

Chinese stir-fry

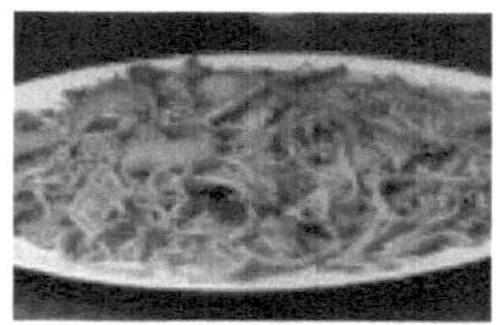

Thai green curry

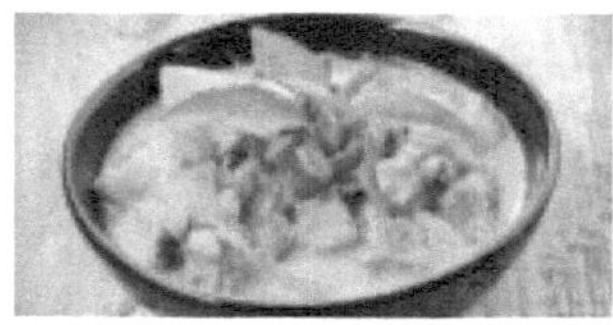

Hot and spicy dish usually made with meat, chicken or fish, and served with rice and noodles.

Sweet and sour chicken

It is a deep-fried chicken served along with the sweet and sour sauce.

Shepherd's pie

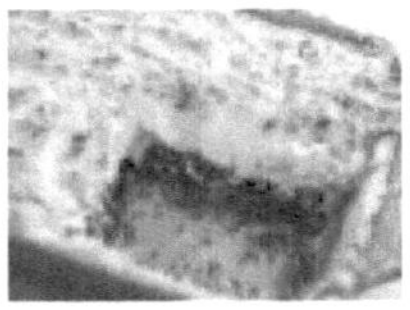

It is a dish lamb and vegetable dish along with mashed potato.

Scotch eggs

It is a boiled egg along with meat sausage meat, and crumbed bread.

Toad-in-the-hole

This dish is made from pudding batter along with vegetables, and gravy.

Banoffee pie

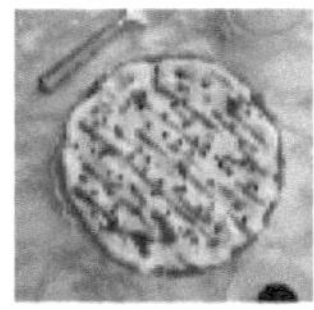

It consists of banana, condensed milk, cream, and toffee.

Middle East

Our global tour is reaching to the Middle East, we should get ready with a pen and diary to make a list of popular foods in this region so that we should not waste time searching for food available here. Don't worry, we are already having this so please follow here and get updated your diary now.

Hummus

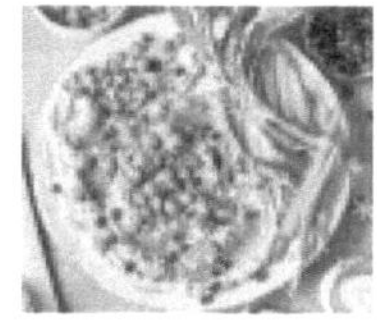

It is a chickpeas spread over hot pita bread.

Grilled halloumi

It is made from milk.
Foul meddamas

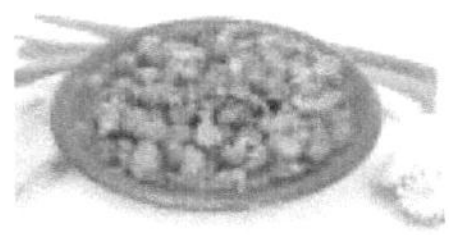

It consisting of fava beans, olive oil, garlic, onion , lemon and parsley.
Falafel

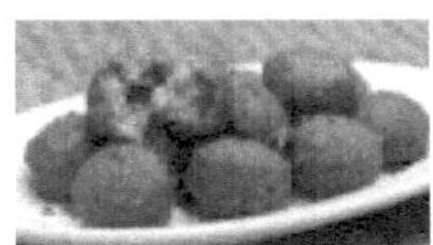

It is a fried chikpeas with some herbs.
Moutabal/baba ghanoush

Eggplant kick added with chili.
Fattoush

Crispy lettuce, crunchy fried squares of pita, diced tomatoes, cucumbers and onion, garlic, lemon, olive oil, and mint.

Umm ali

It is a pastry cooked in milk and cream.
Shanklish

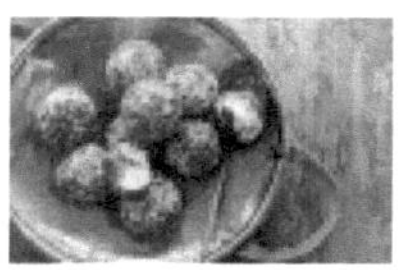

Milk cheese is rolled in zaatar herbs or chili flakes along with tomato and fried onion.

Shawarma

Tender bits of skewered chicken, garlic puree, and salad wrapped in pita

Shish tawook

A chicken dish served with pure garlic paste.

Iraqi masgouf

Slow cooking carp fish and served with lemon and pickle.

Asia & Pacific

Asia and the Pacific are a broad food market globally as it is a highly dense population region, so food consumption is very high here, which demands a range of products to offer. You are excited and love to taste these foods.

Let us first see Indian foods.

India is the biggest country in Asia after China. Diverse cultures, languages, living styles, and food habits exist.

There is a saying in India that after every 100 kilometers, language is got changed and, accordingly, eating habits.

Now, we are here with a summary of the top yummy Indian foods of the country for your ready reference, so when you visit any part of this country, you have a ready-made list of products you must try and taste.

Biryani

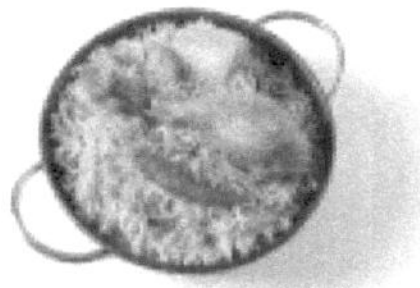

Very popular dish made from mixing rice with meat, eggs, and vegetables, its pure vegetarian version is also available.

Dosa

Pancake is made from fermented rice and black lentil and served with chutney and sambhar.

A varied range of dosas like Masala Dosa, Set Dosa, Uthappam, Paper Dosa, Rava Dosa, 70 mm dosa, Pesarattu, paneer dosa, chicken 65 dosa, cheese dosa, and Pizza Dosaare are available here.

Butter chicken masala

Chicken is dipped in red creamy gravy.

Chat

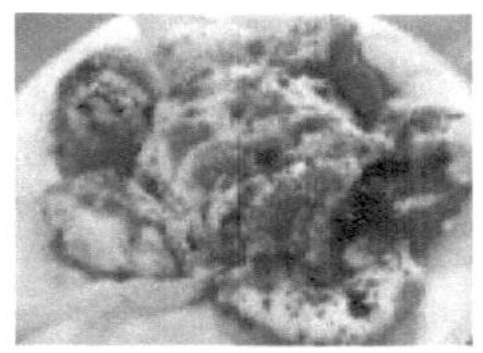

It is made from fried thin chips, potatoes, lentils, puffed rice, chickpeas, yogurt, sliced green chili, mint paste, and onion.

Dhokla

It is a steamed cake made from gram flour, and channadal. It is very spongy and lightweight food.

Idli sambhar

It is a steam rice pancake with coconut paste, and delicious soupy sambhar made from various vegetables, and spices.

Dal Makhani

It is black lentil made with spice and full of butter. A very popular dish in India.

Kichadi

It is made from mixed boiling of split green gram, rice, and spice; once ready and topped with ghee for good taste, it is light when you want to relax your stomach.

Aloo Gobi

It is a vegan dish made from potatoes (i.e., aloo), cauliflower (i.e., gobi), curry leaves, garlic, ginger, coriander, tomato, peas, cumin, and spices.

Rogan josh

It is a trendy dish from the heaven of India that is Kashmir. It is a lamb cooked with gravy from onions, garlic, spices, and ginger.

Tandoori chicken

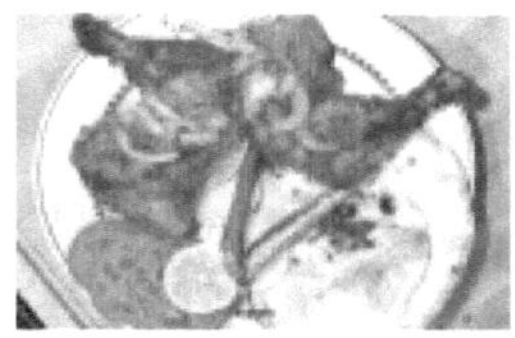

It is a roasted chicken flavored with yogurt & spices.

MalaiKofta

It is a creamy gravy made from tomatoes,cashew nut, and kofta (Gram flour balls fried with vegetables).

Mutter paneer

It is another vegetarian dish. It is a combination of peas, cheese, tomato sauce, and hot spices.

Bhindi masala

It is a spicy ladies's finger, a pure vegan dish.
ChholeBhature

It is made from chickpeas (Chhole), spices, and oil-fried wheat flour bread (Bhature).
Dum aloo

This dish is made from potato cooked in the spicy curry.
GajarkaHalawa

This is a very popular sweet dish made from Carrot, sugar, milk, ghee, and dry fruits like cashew, almond, and cardamom.

Palak Paneer

It is a cheese dipped in spinach paste.

Rajma

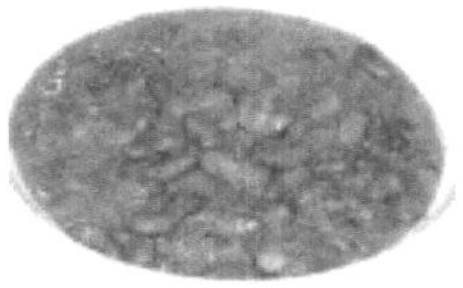

It is a spicy kidney bean.

Chicken 65

It is a deep-fried chicken made with onion, and ginger.

Pongal

It is a fried rice food dish popular in South India.

China

China having many popular food products, here is the list of them for your ready reference :

Sweet and Sour Meat

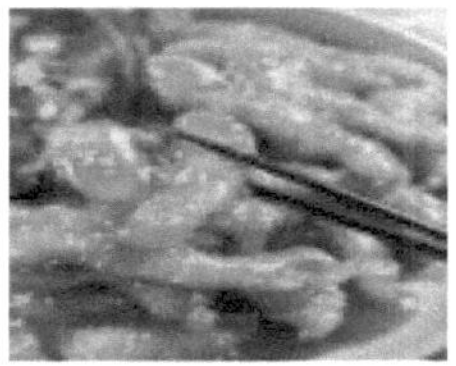

Kung Pao Chicken

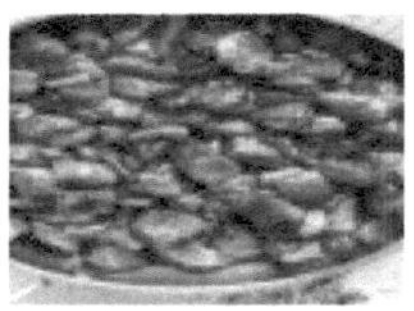

Ma Po Tofu

It consists of tofu, meat, chilies, and pepper.

Dumplings

It is a dough stuffed with stewing mutton, and black pepper.

Wonton

Wonton is filled with cabbage, and minced meat.

Yangzhou (Yeung Chow) Fried Rice

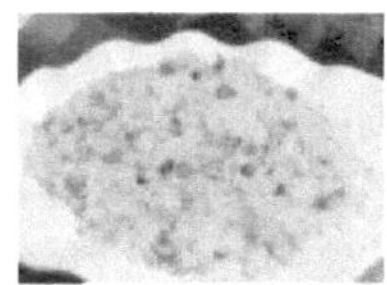

It is a combination of rice ,carrot, beans ,ham sausage, and fried eggs.

Chow Mein

It is basically a fried noodles.

Peking Duck

It is roasted duck meat.

Hot Pot

This dish is made from a stew of meat and vegetables which is cooked in a pot of soup.

Szechwan chili chicken

Chicken is made with white and brown pepper, red n green chili, and ginger.

Veg hakka noodles

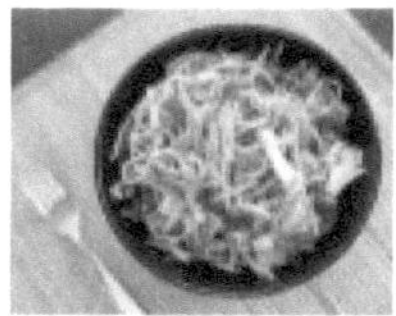

Noodles mixed with capsicum, carrot, spring onions and cabbage with a mix of sauces.

Australia

This country has its product range which they offer to all of us .

Chico rolls

It is a combination of meat stuffed with cabbage, carrot, and onion.
Meat Pie

It is minced meat along with gravy, and tomato sauce.
Chicken Parmigiana

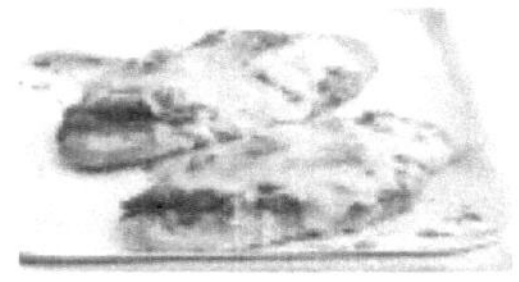

Chicken is topped with tomato sauce, melted cheese and served along with salad, and chips.

Barbequed snags

It is typically a meat sausage wrapped in a slice of bread, and served with fried onion, and sauce.

Barramundi

This is a grilled and fried river fish.

Grilled kangaroo

Pigs in a Blanket

It is a sausage.

Fish n Chips

Most popular food.

Crab sticks

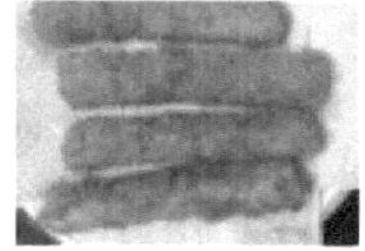

It is a crab leg shape like pieces of fish are dipped in batter, and fried.
>**New Zealand**
>**Hangi**

This dish is made from the meal and vegetables which is slowly cooked in an oven.
>**Crayfish**

It is also known as a lobster.
>**Kina**

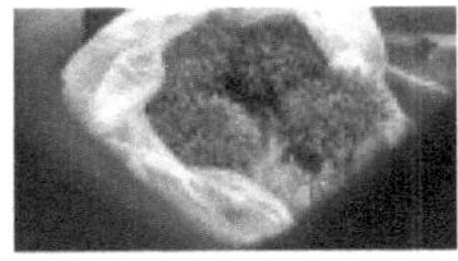

It is a one of seafood in the country.
Whitebait Fritters

This special dish is made from immature fish.
Kumara

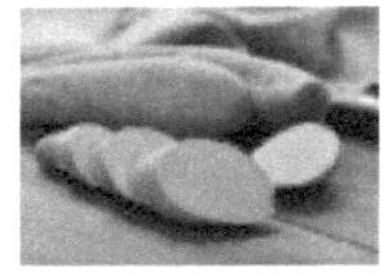

Sweet potato dish.
Roast Lamb

Fish n chip

Meal of fried battered fish, and chips (french fries).

Japan
Gyoza

This is either deep-fried or boiled dish made from garlic chives, Chinese chives, and minced meat.

Sushi

This dish is very popular in Japan made from raw fish over vinegared rice.

Ramen

This is another popular dish consists of bamboo shoots, eggs, chashuu (meat), seaweed and chives.

Tempura

Ingredients for this dish is vegetables and seafood covered in batter, and finally deep-fried.

Yakitori

It is grilled skewered chicken food.

Shabu-Shabu

The main ingredients are sliced meat, vegetables, and sauce.

Yakiniku

It is a grilled meat food and served with a drink.

Thailand

Phat Thai

It's a rice noodle, egg, tofu, and shrimp dish seasoned with fish sauce, sugar, tamarind, vinegar, and chili.

Tom yam

Fatty prawns and a tart/spicy soup in English it is called sour Thai soup.

Laap

It is another Thai food made from minced meat seasoned with roasted rice powder, lime juice, fresh hern, and fish sauce.

Khaosoi

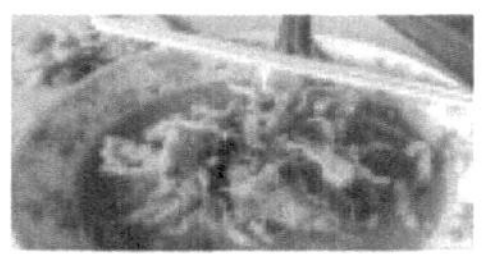

It is a special curry-based noodle soup made from chicken, lime, sliced shallots, and pickled.

Phat kaphrao

Ingredients for a dish is meat flash-fried, holy basil along with chili and garlic.

Yam

This is a spicy Thai 'salad' that combines meat or seafood along with fresh herbs.

Indonesia

NasiGoreng

It's a typical Indonesian fried rice. It consists of meat (usually chicken), vegetables, spices, shallots, garlic, tamarind, and chili and is served with soy sauce and crackers.

Nasicampur

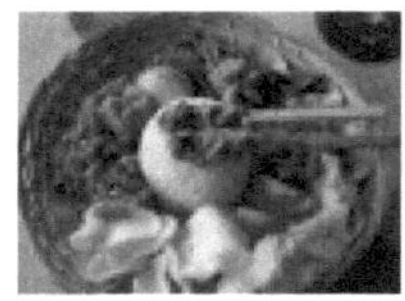

This dish consists of rice mixed with chicken satay, grilled chicken, meat, vegetables, salad, and prawn crackers.

Chicken satay barbecued

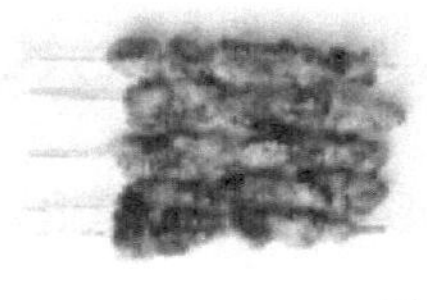

Chicken satay barbecued
Gadogado

It is a salad comprising of vegetables, spicy peanut sauce with fried tofu, and boiled egg.
Sayururap

Blanched vegetable-based salad dressed in shredded coconut.

Back to top

CHAPTER 8

Vegetable Vs Non-vegetable > Which is a better choice

"One cannot think well, love well, sleep well, if not has not dined well."

Verginia Woolf

In this chapter, we have shared comparative for choice between vegetarian and non vegetarian food or vegan food.

Vegetarian & Vegan Vs Non-vegetarian food

The selection of the food as a vegetarian or non-vegetarian depends upon the food habits of individuals and the availability of these foods in that particular geographical region.

The food habits of most of the world are non-vegetarian foods.

These food habits have their advantage and disadvantages.

First, let us understand these categories of foods.

Any food products obtained after killing any animal come under the Non-vegetarian food category.

Vegetarian food has the following categories.

Lacto vegetarian: This consists of plant + dairy products such as milk, ghee, buttermilk, etc.

Ovovegetarian: This consists of plant + egg products.

Ovo Lacto vegetarian: This consists of plant + egg+dairy products such as milk, ghee, buttermilk, etc.

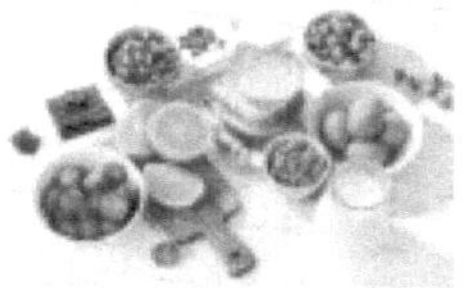

Vegan: This consists of only plant-based products. No animal-based products.

Semi vegetarian: It consists of Ovo Lacto vegetarian plus chicken, and fish products.

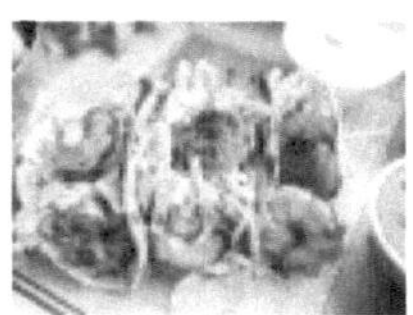

Advantages of non-veg food habits

- It is an excellent source of protein and vitamins.
- It helps in building body and muscle power.
- Fish is a very good source of omega-3.

Disadvantages of non-veg food habits

It enhances the probability of constipation, high blood pressure, obesity, high cholesterol, heart diseases, etc.

It is, as per Indian Ayurveda, non-vegetarian foods are rajasic and task in nature. It reduces the concentration level and promotes anger and lust. It is related to the materialistic world only.

It harms the stomach, liver, and intestine as our body is not made for eating other animal parts as food.

One of the most disappointing facts about eating this type of food is that we are taking the life of a living animal and making it available for food.

In contrast, plants we take in green and dry form, but one plant provides seeds that are the source of hundreds of new vegetable life, and this exponential growth is going on, which means plants never die.

It is not the case with animal foods; after the cruel slaughtering process against the wish of the animal, we make it as food for human consumption when other options are also available.

Dead, dead animal parts can not give birth to a new baby animal; only life can do this.

In some countries, even Dogs and Cats are being grown as livestock for meat food products.

In most countries, these two animals are treated as pet animals and loved with care because of their loyalties to their owner and the natural love they extend to their loved ones.

Can't we think over here and love them as a more precious gift from

nature to us?

Advantage of vegetarian / vegan food habits

- It helps in improving self-control.
- It is low in fats and lowers the risk of heart disease.
- Diets are more balanced
- It is the fiber source needed for our excellent digestion system.
- As per Indian Ayurveda, satvik in nature is related to our noble qualities like a higher level of concentration, peacefulness, love for everyone, and optimism.
- Most vegetable diets are easy to digest compared to non-vegetable diets; doctors recommend light vegetable foods only when you are sick and ask immediately to skip non-vegetable foods until you are fit as earlier.

Many people think that animal food is the primary source of proteins that plants can not provide, but the facts are that all protein is made by plants only.

All plants can take nitrogen from the air and incorporate nitrogen ions in the amino acid, which are transferred to an animal to form animal proteins. Plant protein has more benefits to our physiological structure than animal proteins.

The largest and strongest animal on this earth, like elephants, gorillas, and rhinoceros, are herbivores.

How they get protein to build their strong body is usually argued by many peoples that animal food is the best source of protein to make the body.

Can we think about the other food alternatives (vegetable and milk product base foods) where we can save this innocent and use them more productively for a more extended period?

Note: Not all vegetarians need to be healthy because lifestyle is also an essential factor for your fitness; if you do not take meat but consume high-fat cheese, no physical exercise, and junk food, then it would not be better for them also.

Back to top

CHAPTER 9

WORLD FOOD SAFETY REGULATIONS > Major food regulations

A goal of the food safety professional should be to create food safety culture, not food safety program
   Frank Yiannas
   Global food safety act

In this chapter, we are sharing detailed information on Global food safety act
   <u>**This chapter is comprises of**</u>

- **INTRODUCTION FOOD SAFETY ACT**
- **USFDA**
- **CANADIAN FOOD SAFETY REGULATION**
- **EU REGULATION**
- **REACH**
- **RoHS**
- **GERMAN FOOD SAFETY REGULATION**
- **FRENCH AND ITALIAN FOOD SAFETY REGULATIONS**
- **JAPAN & KOREA SANITATION LAW**
- **CHINA FOOD REGULATION**
- **INDIAN FOOD REGULATION, FSSAI**
- **FOOD ALLERGEN**
- **FOOD COMPLIANCES TESTING INTERNATIONAL LABS**

INTRODUCTION FOOD SAFETY ACT

Food is the basic necessity of every living being on this earth.

Foods have been packed for thousands of years to protect and enhance shelf life.

Until the last century, paper, ceramic, glass, and natural resin were the packaging medium for storing and transporting food items.

In this century, with the invention of synthetic plastic material, the definition of packaging has changed.

With the invention of a wide range of plastics with different inherent properties, it is now possible to protect food from contamination and help enhance the product's shelf life.

Growing awareness for food safety among consumers also raised the bar for the demand for hygienic food; at the same time, in many countries, the government has developed their food safety regulations or adopted other country's or zone regulations to ensure that food reaches to the final consumer are safe without health hazards.

The food and packaging material's safety mainly depends on three critical factors.

These are the toxicity of the substances, migration of substances from packaging material into the food, and the level of exposure of these substances to food.

Standard test methods measure toxicity, while migration depends upon the type of food being packed and consumption by a person based on their eating habits residing in a particular region.

Due to the variation of this pattern, exposure is measured based on an average exposure model covering most of the population.

Some countries are very strict about the packaging system, whereas others rely more on migration data.

Regardless of the individual system, regulations authority consistently enforce standards to implement, and the industry has to comply with the applicable statutory and regulatory requirements.

It is not restricted to the packaging material but also to the equipment and utensils used to prepare food items.

In this chapter, we have provided information on various regulations established in multiple countries worldwide. These regulations include recommendations, legislation, or guidelines.

Many countries regularly update their regulations with new developments; for example, REACH updated their list of substances of high concern every six months and added new substances every time.

It is suggested to visit the respective regulation's website regularly to get recent updates; many rules of some countries are published in the local language only; here, we provide details in English only.

USFDA REGULATION

USFDA (United State Food and Drugs Administration) is an agency under the United States Health and human service Department that looks after the manufacturing and distribution of foods and other food streams of medicine, medical equipment, tobacco, and other consumer products.

Food contact substances

FDA uses the term "indirect food additives" when referring to migrating substances; these have been identified under the umbrella of FCS(food contact substances).

These are the substances intended for use as a part of the material used for manufacturing, packaging, and storing foods but not impacting the final food quality.

Food contact substances are intended for use as a part of materials used in manufacturing, packing, packaging, transporting, or holding food if it does not technically affect the food.

Adhesive, film, ink, and paper are the food-contact substances; all they put together is to make a food-contact material.

The FDA requires clearance for food packaging materials if it complies with the food additive definition as per the FDCA.

FCS has four sections:

- Food additives
- GRAS (Generally Recognized As Safe)
- Prior sanctioned
- Secondary direct additives.

Food Additive Regulations

Regulations are given in CFR (Code of Federal Regulations) under title 21, in "21 CFR – parts 174-186".

Food Contact Notifications (FCN)

Premarket notification for a food contact substance.

It is a Food and Drug Administration Modernization Act 1997 (FDAMA)

21 CFR 170.100 to 170.106.

In 120 days FDA reviews the new user submission.

What could be in FCN.

Indirect food additives, for example, polymers and adjuvants.

Secondary direct additives include ion exchange resins and boiler water additives.

Other non-food additives, for example, GRAS, are antimicrobial. What should not be in FCN.

- Direct food additives
- Carcinogens
- New recycling technology
- Not fulfillment of GMP guidelines

Summary

We are confident that this information has provided a handy overview of regulations applicable in the United States for food packaging material.

We must first determine whether the substance we want to add to our food packaging material is a food additive; if not, if it meets exemption, the substance is not a food additive. If the substance does not fit within the exemption, it is a food additive, and it should be submitted to the FDA for premarket clearance.

CANADA REGULATION

All health and safety standards under the Food and Drug Regulations are implemented by the Canadian Food Inspection Agency (CFIA).

Canadian food law: The following agencies look after the compliances.

Health Canada: This agency formulates the requirement related to health and safety under two rules (i.e., the Food and Drug Act (FDA) and Safe Food for Canadians Act (SFCA)).

Canadian Food Inspection Agency (CFIA): This regulatory body takes care of the health and well-being of humans and animals and the protection of the environment.

Canadian Border Services Agency (CBSA): This agency ensures the security and safety of goods to and from Canada and enforcement of requirements of the FDA, Consumer Packaging and Labeling Act, Canada Meat Inspection, agricultural products, and Fish Inspection Act.

Consumer Packaging and Labelling Act [CPLA]: This act takes care of the packaging, labeling, sale, transportation, advertising of prepackaged and products.

Consumer Packaging and Labeling Regulations [CPLR]: This acts mandates bilingual labeling and units of measurement information.

Food and Drug Regulations [FDR]: This regulation advised the standards for the composition and labeling of food and drugs.

Safe Food for Canadians Act [SFCA]: This act takes care of food commodities, their inspection, labeling, safety, advertising, import, export, and interstate trade, developing standards for them, and other activities related to business.

EU REGULATION

The European Union now has 40 + member states. The EU 2002 established the first food safety law covering the whole food supply chain from farming to your dining table to maintain a high level of food safety and health protection.

Food contact materials play a vital role as they are used in every stage of the supply chain, from manufacturing to storage and transportation; even the food handling system needs to be ensured contamination-free.

These community regulations established are applicable as per framework regulation EC / 1935/2004, and at the same time, specific rules apply to certain materials or substances only.

There are two basic principles, inertness, and safety, upon that legislation on food contact material is based.

This framework regulation EC/1935/2004 is the base legislation that covers all the FCM and articles.

A. Framework regulations 1935/ 2004/EC.

General safety requirements.

There should be no release of harmful substances in the food, which may impact human health.

Food, odor, or taste composition should remain the same at an acceptable level.

There should not be food fraud.

EU authorized to take measures for specific FCMs.

Labeling requirements.

There should be a clear name, address of the producer or seller, instructions, text for food contact or symbol, and language that could be understood.

Traceability system

There should be transparency in the traceability of the final product, right from dispatch detail to raw material vendors, and all records should be made available as and when requested.

Declaration of compliances

For specific measures, the producer should have written documents to confirm the product as per the applicable regulations. In case of the absence of the same, member states can follow national rules for declaration of compliance.

This document as to when and demand should be provided to the competent authority by the supplier.

Safeguard measures

Here, state members can restrict or temporarily suspend authorized FCM and vice versa; the commission could take a call to withdraw the same or adapt some specific legislation.

Good manufacturing practices (GMP)

It covers our quality assurance system, quality control system, and manufacturing practices; we do stringently follow GMP.

It mainly deals with maintaining the hygienic conditions of raw material storage, processing area, equipment, final storage, dispatch area, and supporting services, e.g., Restroom, canteen, change room, personal hygiene, etc.

- EU Measures on specific food contact material (FCM)
- EU 10/2011 regulations for plastic materials.
- EU regulation 282/2008 for recycled plastic material.
- Regulation 450/2009/EC for active and intelligent material.
- Ceramic directives(84/500/EEC) for a limit on Pb and Cd migration.
- Directive 2007/42/EC directives for regenerated cellulose. Uncoated or coated with a plastic coating, this should comply with EU 10/2011 directives.
- Epoxy derivatives regulations Regulation 1895/2005/EC) for NODGE, BFDGE, BADGE, etc.
- Nitrosamines(Directive 93/11/EC) and their release limitations.

EU regulation when the material is not covered by directives materials is suggested to follow resolution Resap (Policy statement) no legal.

- Resolution ResAP(2004) 5 for silicone
- Resolution ResAP(2004) 4 for rubber
- Resolution ResAP(2004) 1 for paper and board material
- Resolution ResAP(2004) 1 for coating

The most common required testing in the EU market

Global migration testing: This test comprises different simulant(s) and specific temperature and time testing conditions.

- Distilled water
- 3% Acetic acid
- 15% Ethanol
- 50% Ethanol
- 95% Ethanol
- Iso-octane
- Rectified olive oil
- SML (Specific Migration Limit): This test applies to the unique substance.
- Acrylonitrile
- Bisphenol A
- Formaldehyde
- Nitrosamines
- Melamines
- Caprolactam
- Total content test – residual test
- Heavy metals
- VOC (Volatile Organic Compound)
- Vinyl chloride
- Phthalates
- Isocyanates

DOC(Declaration Of Compliances)

According to EC 1935/ 2004, the manufacturer or distributor has to submit a DOC of the product or material directly coming into contact with food.

To issue such a declaration, supporting test results should comply with EC 1935/ 2004 and include its directives in DOC.

GERMAN LFGB

This food contact materials legislation (German food, feed, and commodity law) is the same as EU directives 1935/ 2004/EC.

LFGB Regulation section 30 prohibits material that directly comes into contact with food and is endangered to human beings due to toxicity or impurity in the material.

LFGB Regulation section 31 prohibits bringing material into direct contact with food.

LFGB Regulation section 33 prohibits misleading information on products the supplier shares.

BFR (Germany's Federal Risk Assessment Institute) has implemented EU directives nationally.

Material not covered in EU directives is taken into BFR plastic standard for evaluation. It considers (but is not restricted to) Silicone, rubber, paper & paper board material, and polymers.

FRENCH DGCRF

French has its national food regulation- Decree 2007-766, the same as EU directives 1935/ 2004/EC.

To prove compliance with regulations, It provides the following directives

Arretes du 02/01/2003 for plastic material

Arretes du 13/01/1976 for stainless steel.

Arretes du 25/11/1992 for Silicons.

It includes 2002/72/EC & 84/500/EEC and other EC directive requirements.

When the material is not covered under Arretes

DGCCRF (General Directorate for Competition Policy, Consumer Affair and Fraud Control, national authority) information notice 2004/64 compilation of French regulations & requirements on FCM on a national level.

ITALIAN REGULATION

Italy has its national food regulation- Italian Legislative Decree 777-1982, the same as EU directives 1935/ 2004/EC.

To prove compliance with regulations ministerial decree provides the following directives.

Ministerial decree 21/03/1973

Ministerial decree 04/04/1985

Ministerial decree 18/04/2007

Some material covered under DM 21/03/1973 is Plastic, rubber, paper & paper board material, regenerated cellulose, glass, and stainless steel.

The Plastic requirement aligns with 2002/72/EC directives.

JAPAN & KOREA SANITATION ACT

JAPAN

In Japan, food contact materials are regulated under the Japan Food sanitation act no. 233, 1947.

Materials are getting tested as per the notice no. MHLW 370/ 1959 "Specification and standards for food and food additives".

Testing performed under this standard are for total lead and cadmium, Heavy metals as lead, consumption of Potassium permanganate, evaporation residue, other material, and specific migration testing.

KOREA

In Korea, food contact materials are regulated under the Korean Food sanitation act no. 3823 10th May 1986 and its subsequent amendments.

Testing performed in this act is the same as Japan.

REACH REGULATION

REACH

The European REACH Regulation (Registration, Evaluation, Authorization, and Restriction of Chemicals) 1907/2006 ensures that to know more about new chemicals being used in the EU and restrict the use of these chemicals, which may negatively affect human health or the environment.

Applicable for:

The substances regulation applies to all the products sold in Europe.

Requirements:

- Suppliers must inform customers if any of the listed Substances of Very High Concern are present in products/ parts with a concentration of more than 0.1% weight/weight.
- The list is updated every six months, mainly in Dec/ Jan and Jun/ Jul month.
- Key agencies part of REACH
- The European Chemicals Agency (ECHA).

The UK Competent Authority (CA) is located within the Health and Safety Executive (HSE), responsible for the day-to-day running of REACH in the UK.

RoHS DIRECTIVES

RoHS

This is the European RoHS Directive on the Restriction of the use Of Hazardous Substances in Electrical and Electronic Equipment (EEE), which may adversely affect human health and the environment as well as sound recovery and disposal of waste EEE.

Many countries have implemented similar regulations the same as REACH and RoHS.

Applicable for

This regulation is applicable to all the electrical and electronic equipment and products have an electronic component sold in Europe and having the possibility to be sold in Europe.

Requirements

- According to this Directive required to eliminate the

following contents from their products

- Lead (0.1%*),
- Mercury (0.1%*),
- Cadmium (0.01%*),
- Hexavalent chromium (0.1%*),
- PBBs (0.1%*),
- PBDEs (0.1%*)
- DEHP (0,1%*),
- BBP (0,1%*),
- DBP (0,1%*)
- DIBP (0,1%*)

* Indicates maximum concentration values tolerated by weight in homogeneous materials.

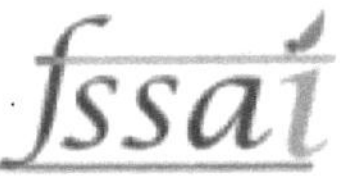

INDIAN REGULATION

The FSSAI is a statutory body under the Food Safety and Standards Act, 2006.

FSS Act, 2006 consolidates various acts & orders that were handled by multiples departments, these are as under:

- Prevention of Food Adulteration Act, 1954
- Fruit Products Order, 1955
- Meat Food Products Order, 1973
- Vegetable Oil Products (Control) Order, 1947
- Edible Oils Packaging (Regulation) Order 1988
- Milk and Milk Products Order, 1992
- Key functions of FSSAI are as below
- Setting standards of food products
- Developing safe food practices

- Licensing food businesses
- Ensure compliance through inspections
- Testing foods for standards
- Training and building capacity
- Citizens Outreach

CHINA REGULATION

A wide range of regulations are implemented in China to ensure the safety of human beings who consume food products.

China food safety regulations:

This regulation established the responsibility of producers and business operators for food safety during storage, transportation of food products, and food fraud management of specific food.

China food additive regulations:

Approved food additives list is given under regulation GB 2760-2011. Food additives should not be used to cover product deficiency or to produce degraded food products.

China food contact material & Food packaging material regulation:

(FCMs) are regulated by the China Food Safety Law with the latest updates.

Article 32 & 62 of this law restricts the importation, use, or purchasing of food-related products which do not comply with food safety standards.

China food law and regulation:

China state council published regulations on food safety law dated 31st Oct'19. It includes detailed rules for food surveillance, assessment, safety, inspection, import, export, etc.

China label regulation:

All imported foods and beverages must have a label, mostly in white color and written in Chinese characters. The label must be approved by CIQ (China Entry-Exit Inspection and Quarantine Bureau).

China food import regulation:

All imports are classified under three categories: prohibited, restricted, and permitted. Vendors looking to import food first need to get a license from the government and registration with CAA (Certification and Accreditation Administration).

FOOD ALLERGENS

Food safety is a significant global challenge; we have every aspect in detail in our other book, food safety challenges; food allergen is one of these challenges.

The European Union has prepared a list of allergens that are identified as Wheat, rye, barley, hazelnuts, walnuts, cashews, pecan nuts, oats, spelt, kamut, crustaceans, eggs, fish, peanuts, soybeans, milk, nuts, for example, almonds, pistachio nuts, Brazil nuts, macadamia nuts, Queensland nuts, mustard, and sesame seeds.

Japan has declared allergens; these are salmon roe, soybean, kiwi, banana eggs, milk, dairy products, wheat, buckwheat, shrimp/prawn, peanuts, crab, chicken, tree nuts, squid, mackerel, meat, salmon, gelatin yam, and peach.

Canada has listed the top 10 allergens: milk, eggs, mustard, peanuts, seafood (fish, crustaceans, shellfish), soy, Sesame, Soy, tree nuts, wheat, and sulfites.

INTERNATIONAL FOOD COMPLIANCE TESTING LAB

There are many certified international accredited labs those test products for its different global food regulations compliance.

- Intertek lab
- SGS lab
- TUV Nord
- TUV Sud
- TÜV Rheinland
- Eurofins
- AGQ Labs
- CFTRI, India
- Analytical Food Laboratories (AFL), US
- QIMA
- CCIC Europe
- RPS Laboratories
- V Trust Inspection services
- NSF
- ARBRO

Back to top

Epilogue

My lovely dear friends and passionate readers,

I am highly grateful to you for spending a perfect quality time reading this one unique book on altogether different kinds of genres right from the beginning till the end.

I hope this was an excellent experience for you.

I captured various dimensions of FMCG (Fast Moving Consumer Goods), a range of continental foods, hygiene practices, and international food safety regulations from different perspectives.

I'd written this book considering that global traveling is frequent nowadays and the high probability of having unhealthy foods.

Different country has different food culture; it may suit or may not suit everyone.

I have given the composition of every food product, which would help my food lovers and travelers select food conveniently.

Hygiene practices explained may feel uncomfortable to some, but it will give a second thought to think over there. There is no compulsion.

Various international food safety regulations will help to understand the gravity of food safety and approaches by different countries to ensure the good health of everyone.

We see everything in this world very simply, but to understand each, you should have different glasses to this highly complex world.

It was an effort to say a lot with a few words.

I explained all concepts in a familiar, easy-to-understand layman's language for my global reader.

I will wait for your valuable feedback to make this book more exciting, and informative. If you find some amendment are required,

I shall be back with updated version, and more interesting information; due to some constraints, I couldn't become part of this first edition, but, in a short duration, this would be part of the second edition.

Thanks a lot.

I am reachable at my Email: manish260470@gmail.com

Don't miss out!

Visit the website below and you can sign up to receive emails whenever Manish Sharma publishes a new book. There's no charge and no obligation.

https://books2read.com/r/B-A-IZTZ-JVCNC

BOOKS 2 READ

Connecting independent readers to independent writers.

Did you love *One Minute Food Manager*? Then you should read *Funny Stories Good Luck Bad Luck*[1] by Manish Sharma!

[2]

Everyone on this earth has gone through various phases of life right from their childhood to final destiny. This journey of life brought them many bitter and sweeter experiences, those with a passage of time in later stage of life seems to be of very funny moments, and you started laughing on yourself. This is the tragedy that bitter experience is always more frequent than sweeter experience and always teach us a lesson. Each one of us feels great when remembers old memories of the life and would like to live past life time and again. It is just like a beautiful dream you have seen once and wanted to recur. This book is all about those small funny life events, where every moment was so powerful to change your final destiny and you were not aware about this or realize

---

1. https://books2read.com/u/bW6ZOW

2. https://books2read.com/u/bW6ZOW

it. It is a combination of science, management principles, spirituality, emotions, morality, and social science explained in a funny way. It is sure that you can't decide your destiny as per your will or wish, surrounding circumstances at that time decide your life path and you have to only follow them. Situation at that time may encourage or discourage you but in later stage you will realize that was the only best possible way. This book is a collection of small funny stories, and I believe that each one of you will really enjoy reading this book till the last page.

Hide Long Description

Read more at https://excellence2fmcg.com/.

Also by Manish Sharma

Funny Stories Good Luck Bad Luck
One Minute Food Manager

Watch for more at https://excellence2fmcg.com/.